INTELLECTUAL PROPERTY

Update Service

BECOME A SUBSCRIBER

Did you purchase this product from a bookstore?

BECOME A SUBSCRIBER

Did you purchase this product from a bookstore?

If you did, it's important for you to become a subscriber. John Wiley & Sons, Inc. may publish, on a periodic basis, supplements and new editions to reflect the latest changes in the subject matter that you ***need to know*** in order to stay competitive in this ever-changing industry. By contacting the Wiley office nearest you, you'll receive any current update at no additional charge. In addition, you'll receive future updates and revised or related volumes on a 30-day examination review.

If you purchased this product directly from John Wiley & Sons, Inc., we have already recorded your subscription for this update service.

To become a subscriber, please call **1-877-762-2974** or send your name, company name (if applicable), address, and the title of the product to:

mailing address:	**Supplement Department** **John Wiley & Sons, Inc.** **10475 Crosspoint Blvd.** **Indianapolis, IN 46256**
e-mail:	**subscriber@wiley.com**
fax:	**1-800-605-2665**
online:	www.wiley.com

For customers outside the United States, please contact the Wiley office nearest you:

Professional & Reference Division
John Wiley & Sons Canada, Ltd.
90 Eglinton Ave. E. Suite 300
Toronto, Ontario M4P 2Y3
Canada
Phone: 416-236-4433
Phone: 1-800-567-4797
Fax: 416-236-8743
Email: canada@wlley.com

John Wiley & Sons Australia, Ltd.
42 McDougall Street
Milton, Queensland 4064
AUSTRALIA
Phone: 61-7-3859-9755
Fax: 61-7-3859-9715
Email: aus-custservice@wiley.com

John Wiley & Sons, Ltd.
European Distribution Centre
New Era Estate
Oldlands Way
Bognor Regis, West Sussex
PO22 9NQ, UK
Phone: (0)1243 779777
Fax: (0)1243 843 123
Email: customer@wlley.co.uk

John Wiley & Sons (Asia) Pte., Ltd.
1 Fusionopolis Walk
#07-01 Solaris South Tower
SINGAPORE 138628
Phone: 65-6302-9838
Fax: 65-6265-1782
Customer Service: 65-6302-9800
Email: asiacart@wiley.com

5TH EDITION

INTELLECTUAL PROPERTY

VALUATION, EXPLOITATION, AND INFRINGEMENT DAMAGES

2019 CUMULATIVE SUPPLEMENT

RUSSELL L. PARR

WILEY

Published by John Wiley & Sons, Inc., Hoboken, New Jersey.

Published simultaneously in Canada.

For general information on our other products and services, or technical support, please contact our Customer Care Department within the United States at 800-762-2974, outside the United States at 317-572-3993 or fax 317-572-4002.

Wiley also publishes its books in a variety of electronic formats. Some content that appears in print may not be available in electronic books.

For more information about Wiley products, visit our web site at www.wiley.com.

Library of Congress Cataloging-in-Publication Data:

ISBN 9781119356219 (cloth); ISBN 9781119538202 (supplement)
ISBN 9781119538240 (epub)
ISBN 9781119538233 (ePDF)

Cover Design: Wiley

Printed in the United States of America

V10008254_021419

ABOUT THE AUTHOR

Russell L. Parr is President of IPRA, Inc. He is an expert at determining the value and royalty rate pricing of intellectual property.

For over 30 years, Russell has completed complex consulting assignments involving the valuation and pricing of patents, trademarks, copyrights, and other intangible assets. His opinions are used to accomplish licensing transactions, acquisitions, transfer pricing, litigation support, collateral-based financing, and joint ventures. Russell also has served as an expert witness regarding patented technology infringement damages and has testified at trial or deposition over 70 times. Past assignments have included the valuation of the Dr. Seuss copyrights and the patent portfolio of AT&T. Russell has also conducted valuations and royalty rate studies for pharmaceuticals, semiconductor process and product technology, agricultural technology, automotive battery technology, biotechnology, camera technology, chemical formulations, communications technology, computer software, cosmetics, consumer and corporate trademarks, drug delivery systems, flowers, incinerator feed systems, lasers, medical instrument technology, motivational book copyrights.

Russell has authored or co-authored 10 books published by John Wiley & Sons. His books have translated into Japanese, Korean, Italian, Chinese, Romanian, and Russian. His flagship book is *Intellectual Property: Valuation, Exploitation and Infringement Damages*, fifth edition.

Russell also publishes, through IPRA, Inc., three royalty rate resource books, which have been sold all over the world. These books are dedicated to reporting detailed information about the economic aspects of intellectual property transactions including licensing. The titles are *Royalty Rates for Technology*, sixth edition; *Royalty Rates for Trademarks & Copyrights*, fifth edition; and *Royalty Rates for Pharmaceuticals & Biotechnology*, eighth edition.

Russell has a master's in business administration from Rutgers University (1981); and a bachelor of science in electrical engineering from Rutgers University (1976). His professional designations include Chartered Financial Analyst (CFA), Accredited Senior Appraiser (ASA), and Certified Licensing Professional (CLP). He is a member of the Licensing Executives Society and on the advisory board of three professional publications, *Licensing Economics Review*, *IP Litigator*, and *The Licensing Journal.* Russell is also on the Advisory Board Member of Innovation Asset Group, a company developing enterprise software for intellectual property management. He also served on the Intangible Asset Valuation Standards Committee of the American Society of Appraisers.

CONTENTS

PREFACE

This is the first supplement to the fifth edition of *Intellectual Property: Valuation, Exploitation and Infringement Damages*. It contains the following chapters.

CHAPTER 2A—SCANDALOUS TRADEMARKS

A new category of trademarks has emerged from the courts. Section 2(a) of the Lanham Act says that the USPTO may refuse to register any trademark that "consists of or comprises immoral, deceptive, or scandalous matter; or matter which may disparage or falsely suggest a connection with persons, living or dead, institutions, beliefs, or national symbols, or bring them into contempt or disrepute." Recently, the U.S. Supreme Court struck down the Lanham Act's disparagement clause as unconstitutional in *Matal v. Tam*.[1]

CHAPTER 3A – ASSEMBLED WORK FORCES ARE VALUABLE BUT MAYBE NOT THE CHIEF EXECUTIVE OFFICER

The chief executive officer (CEO) is the most expensive employee at a company. Their pay packages can include pay, bonuses, shares of stock, and stock options. Boards of Directors try to tie CEO compensation to company and share price performance, but the results do not always work out. This new section presents evidence that CEOs are often over-rewarded for marginal company performance. When valuing an assembled workforce, special considerations are needed when considering the CEO.

CHAPTER 16A—ROYALTY RATES FOR LICENSING, DATA SOURCES

This chapter provides information about resources that are available for discovering royalty rate data that can serve as guidance for use in licensing agreements.

1. 137 S. Ct. 1744 (June 19, 2017).

CHAPTER 27A—*EXMARK* ESTABLISHES NEW ROYALTY DAMAGES MODEL

In *Exmark Manufacturing Company v. Briggs & Stratton Power*, the U.S. Court of Appeals for the Federal Circuit approved a reasonable royalty damages theory based on the total value of an accused product, even though the patented invention was only part of a multicomponent product. Previously, apportionment was handled at the royalty base. Now, the entire value of the product can be used as the base, and apportionment can be handled with an appropriate royalty rate.

APPENDIX C-1—FOOD & BEVERAGE INDUSTRY ROYALTY RATES AND SUPPORT FROM THE 25% RULE

Royalty rate data from *Royalty Rates for Trademarks & Copyrights*, published by IPRA, Inc. is reported along with a discussion of the state of the food and beverage industry. Generally, the food and beverage industry is very competitive resulting in thin profit margins and royalty rates for food & beverage trademarks reflect the low profit margins with low royalty rates. This supplemental chapter presents a discussion about the stresses in the food and beverage industry along with royalty rates found in the industry. In some cases, relatively high royalty rates are being paid, even in an industry known for low profit margins. This may be a sign of desperation as industry participants attempt to reshape their companies and address new and fundamental shifts in the marketplace.

The data presented in this new section is then compared to royalty rates indicated from application of the 25% Rule.

INTELLECTUAL PROPERTY

CHAPTER **2A**

SCANDALOUS TRADEMARKS

As previously discussed in the main text on page 29, a trademark is used to identify the source of a product or service and to distinguish that product or service from those coming from other sources. As defined in the Trademark Act of 1946 (the Lanham Act), a trademark is "any word, name, symbol or device or any combination thereof used by someone to identify and distinguish his goods, including a unique product, from those manufactured or sold by others and to indicate the source of the goods. . . ." A trademark also serves as an assurance of quality—the consumer comes to associate a level of quality with the goods or services bearing a given trademark. Trademarks have been described as the embodiment of goodwill. They convey product characteristics such as quality, value, safety, and prestige.

Not every word or symbol is acceptable as a trademark. Geographic names or surnames generally cannot be registered, and the same is true of commonly used words for an object or good, such as "knife," "cotton," or "cup." Marks that would be misleading (vis-à-vis the intended goods or services), or those in poor taste are not registrable. Trademarks are categorized as follows:

Fanciful Marks. These are words that are made up and have no built-in meaning, such as XFINITY, VERIZON, LEXUS, and CHEERIOS.

Arbitrary Marks. These are existing words with no relation to the goods or services with which they are associated, such as APPLE (computers), SHELL (petroleum products), WINDOWS (software), or NIKE (sportswear).

Suggestive Marks. These are words that suggest some attribute of or benefit from the goods or services, but do not describe the goods themselves, such as COPPERTONE (tanning lotion), CATERPILLAR (tractors), or WHIRLPOOL (washers).

Descriptive Marks. These describe the goods or services or a characteristic of them. They cannot be protected until they have achieved distinctiveness through use and advertising, which is called acquiring "secondary meaning." Examples are CARFRESHENER for an auto deodorizer, RICH 'N CHIPS for chocolate chip cookies, or the descriptor GOLD MEDAL for flour or BLUE RIBBON for beer.

Generic Marks. These are the weakest types of "marks" (and cannot even qualify as "marks" in the legal sense) and are never registrable or enforceable against third parties. Because generic words are the common, everyday name for goods and services and everyone has the right to use such terms to refer to their goods and services, they are not protectable. An example would be to try to register the mark BICYCLE to use in the bicycle business.

Trademarks are used to identify goods. Many common trademarks are some form of the owning company's name, usually in a distinctive type style, or a logo. Examples are IBM, GM, GE, GOODYEAR, and AT&T.

LATHAM ACT DISPARAGEMENT CLAUSE IS STRUCK DOWN

Section 2(a) of the Lanham Act says that the U.S. Patent Office (USPTO) may refuse to register any trademark that "consists of or comprises immoral, deceptive, or scandalous matter; or matter that may disparage or falsely suggest a connection with persons, living or dead, institutions, beliefs, or national symbols, or bring them into contempt or disrepute." Recently, the U.S. Supreme Court struck down the Lanham Act's disparagement clause as unconstitutional in *Matal v. Tam,* 137 S. Ct. 1744 (June 19, 2017). The case involved an Asian-American dance-rock band named The Slants. who sought to register their band name as a trademark. The U.S. Patent and Trademark Office rejected the band's application to register its name under Section 2(a) of the Lanham Act. The case made its way to the Supreme Court, which struck down the disparagement clause as viewpoint discrimination in violation of the First Amendment's free speech clause.

Since this decision the Washington Redskins football team and the D*kes on Bikes Women's Motorcycle Contingent have prevailed in their federal trademark registration disputes. Another trademark application deemed questionable was recently approved for CH*NKY MINKY FRIENDS FOREVER. Another win was recorded by SLANT'D, the name of a magazine that celebrates Asian American identity on July 10, 2018.

SOME IMMORAL AND SCANDALOUS TRADEMARKS STILL FIGHT FOR REGISTRATION

Eric Brunetti founded FUCT in 1990, and the brand's clothing is distributed by stores like Urban Outfitters. In 2011, Brunetti sought to register the FUCT mark with the USPTO. The USPTO rejected the application. FUCT was looked at as the past tense of the verb "f*ck," and was deemed vulgar. Brunetti's case eventually made its way to the U.S. Court of Appeals for the Federal Circuit. The Federal Circuit in the Brunetti case wrote, "independent of whether the immoral or scandalous provision is viewpoint discriminatory, we conclude the provision impermissibly discriminates based on the content in violation of the First Amendment."[1] The next step is the U.S. Supreme Court. Meanwhile, the USPTO continues to receive applications for questionable trademarks. Such applications are pending including: Applications to register several other variations of the word "f*ck" have been suspended, such as AMERICAN AS F*CK, TEAM F*CK YOU, and JUST F*CK IT.

Also awaiting a Supreme Court decision in Brunetti are applications to register variations of the word "c*nt" including two related to

1. Brian Iverson, "Disparaging, Immoral, and Scandalous Trademarks Since Matal v. Tam," IP Watchdog, August 11, 2018, http://www.ipwatchdog.com/2018/08/11/disparaging-immoral-scandalous-trademarks-matal-tam/id=100179/.

campaigns to prevent texting and driving (C*NT: CAN U NOT TEXT and IF YOU TEXT AND DRIVE YOU'RE A C*NT).

OUTSTANDING CONSTITUTIONAL SCRUTINY AND STATUTORY INTERPRETATION QUESTIONS

Are trademarks considered "commercial speech"? If so, laws relating to trademarks might be subject to relaxed scrutiny for constitutional compliance rather than strict scrutiny.

While *Matal v. Tam* adds another category to the list of trademarks, we are not likely going to see a rush on the USPTO for the registration of scandalous trademarks. Most companies are trying to attract the attention of a wide-ranging audience and any trademark that might offend the politically correct marketplace will not be desirable.

CHAPTER 3A

ASSEMBLED WORK FORCES ARE VALUABLE BUT MAYBE NOT THE CHIEF EXECUTIVE OFFICER

An assembled workforce is the existing collection of employees that permits a company to operate at peak efficiency. Without a well-trained and knowledgeable collection of employees all of the assets of a company sit idle. Without employees, no one is manning the computers in accounts receivable to make sure customers are making timely payments. Manufacturing equipment may be humming with electrical energy, but no one is making sure that raw materials, subassemblies, and final products are zooming through the manufacturing facility. No one is inventing new products, developing marketing campaigns, calling on new customers or handling human resources questions. Without an assembled workforce nothing happens. No profits. No investment rate of return.

When an acquirer sets up an opening balance sheet for an acquired entity, the acquirer is required by accounting standards to record the fair value of the assets acquired and liabilities assumed. The premium paid—which is equal to the purchase price in excess of the acquired net tangible assets' fair value—must first be attributed to the fair value of identifiable intangible assets, such as customer lists and relationships, contracts, patents, and trademarks. Any excess premium is then recorded as goodwill.

An assembled workforce is not itself an identifiable intangible asset. But an assembled workforce may affect the value of identifiable intangible assets. When an acquirer uses an excess earnings method to place values on identifiable intangible assets, the cash flows from the asset are often reduced by a contributory asset charge for the value of the assembled workforce. This asset charge is essentially an expense for the use of the workforce that contributes to the realization of the value. The charge reduces the net income expected to be realized from the identifiable intangible asset and therefore, the value attributed to these assets.

The assembled workforce asset charge is based on the value of an assembled workforce, measured as the cost to recruit and train a workforce to replace the existing service capacity of the acquired one. These calculations often have limitations.

Consider one of the most expensive employees a company possesses—the chief executive officer (CEO). These individuals are the highest paid employees at almost all companies. They determine the strategic direction of a company and then drive all other executives and employees to execute their plan.

It is common to think of these employees as the most important, but studies show this assumption may be wrong.

The *New York Times* published data of the 200 of the highest-paid chief executives in American business. The data comes from the Equilar 200 Highest-Paid CEO Rankings, which lists the compensation of 200 chief executives of public companies with annual revenue of at least $1 billion. The data was for the year ended 2017.[1]

The chart below shows the poor relationship between the top 100 CEO compensation packages and the performance of their company's share price for 2017. CEO compensation is a combination of salary, bonus, perks, stock, and options.

A positive 20% return can be obtained by paying a CEO over $100 million. The chart also shows the same performance and even more can be obtained from CEOs being provided a $20 million compensation package. While it would have nice to see higher performance associated with higher compensation, the chart doesn't even come close to showing such a relationship.

1. "The Highest-Paid C.E.O.s in 2017," *New York Times*, May 25, 2018, https://www.nytimes.com/interactive/2018/05/25/business/ceo-pay-2017.html.

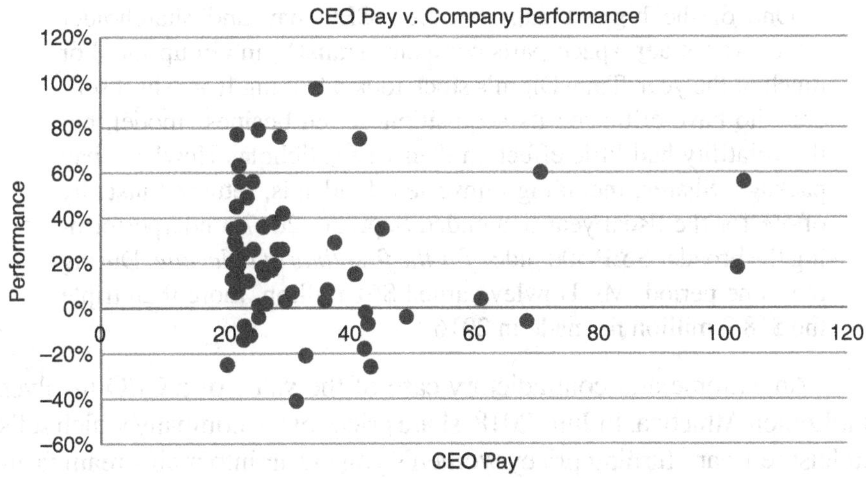

Corporate boards continue to try to tie CEO pay to company performance. Specifically, they want CEO pay to reflect improved company performance and shareholder returns. Great performance equals great pay. Poor performance equals lower pay and often the ouster of the CEO. In reality, CEO pay and performance often don't match up.

Speaking about CEO pay and company performance, Herman Aguinis, a professor of management at George Washington University School of Business told the *Wall Street Journal*, "Stars are often underpaid, while average performers are often overpaid."[2] In support of this statement, the *Wall Street Journal* cited the following:

> CBS Corp. paid its chief, Leslie Moonves, $69.3 million last year; total shareholder return was negative 6.2%. His pay was virtually unchanged from $69.6 million in 2016 when the broadcaster achieved a one-year return of 37%.
>
> Allergan PLC's Brent Saunders received a 700% raise in 2017 to $32.8 million, despite total shareholder return of negative 21%. The compensation package came during a year when Allergan ran into patent setbacks for one of its best sellers, dry-eye drug Restasis, which contributed to a 22% drop in the firm's share price for the year.

2. Vanessa Fuhrmans, "CEO Pay and Performance Often Don't Match Up," *Wall Street Journal*, May 14, 2018, https://www.wsj.com/articles/ceo-pay-and-performance-dont-match-up-1526299200.

> One of the biggest gaps between CEO pay and shareholder return was at aerospace-parts company TransDigm Group Inc. For much of the year, TransDigm's stock took a beating from short sellers who have criticized its acquisition-driven business model, but the volatility had little effect on then-CEO Nicholas Howley's pay package. Shares, including reinvested dividends, returned just shy of 5% for the fiscal year that ended Sept. 30, 2017, underperforming the broader S&P 500 index *for the first time in a decade*. During the same period, Mr. Howley earned \$61 million, more than triple the \$18.9 million he made in 2016.[3]

An extreme and contradictory case of the value of a CEO involves LuluLemon Athletica. In June 2018, share prices of the company which sells "athleisure wear," turning pricey women's yoga wear into mainstream fashion, were up nearly 15.5 percent at \$121.26. This happened without a CEO.

CEO Laurent Potdevin had a multi-year relationship with a female designer at the company he oversaw. This was one of the issues that caused his departure from the company on February 5, 2018. A company statement indicated that Potdevin, "fell short of . . . standards of conduct." LuluLemon did not find a replacement for the CEO job until July 2018, but during the interim the company prospered and the company share price soared.

It can be argued that the strategic plan Potdevin put in place leading up to his departure fueled LuluLemon's success, but this brings up the question about the need for a high-paid CEO. Once a strategic plan is established, is there a need for a highly-paid CEO? Companies may find that temporarily employing a strategic planning consultant to establish a plan, then leaving execution to other employees can serve just as well as employing a high-priced centerpiece for the long haul.

When considering the value of CEOs as part of an assembled workforce, their value may not be indicated by their compensation package unless it is supported by shareholder returns.

KEY PERSONNEL CAN BITE YOU IN YOUR SHARE PRICE

The private actions of key company personnel have also had significant impact on company share prices. Sexual harassment accusations and other offensive behaviors have recently strained company share prices,

3. Ibid.

further bringing into question the value of key personnel to a company. Consider the results of recent questionable behaviors by key personnel.

POOR LANGUAGE BY PAPA JOHN'S CEO COST INVESTORS 43% IN STOCK VALUE. John H. Schnatter is the founder of Papa John International, Inc. He assumed the position of *Papa John* and was featured on national television commercials for the business. The company slogan is *Better Ingredients, Better Pizza.* Schnatter stepped down as CEO on January 1, 2018, after comments he made criticizing National Football League commissioner Roger Goodell for not doing anything about national anthem protests.

In late 2016, some NFL players had started to kneel before the start of a game during the playing of the national anthem. The protests by players about racial injustice were divisive. While many people across the country, especially NFL fans, acknowledged the players rights to protest, they also strongly felt that kneeling during the national anthem was beyond inappropriate. Members of the military and veterans thought the move by the players was disrespectful to their sacrifices. NFL leadership found itself in an impossible position and were slow to take a stand on the issue and even slower to develop a compromise.

In the fall of 2017, Schnatter, then-CEO of Papa John's, blamed the company's poor quarterly earnings report on the "controversy," saying it was an aftereffect of the league's "poor leadership" and "should have been nipped in the bud a year and a half ago."[4] Papa John had been the NFL's official pizza sponsor since 2010 and advertised heavily during games. The company reacted to Schnatter's statement by removing him as CEO on January 1, 2018.

Another scandal broker broke out over use by Schnatter of a racial slur during a conference call. While trying to minimize controversy over other politically charged comments. Schnatter latter asserted that Colonel Sanders had used the slur and it had not affected his popularity. Schnatter also apologized for the slur, saying it was "inappropriate and hurtful."

Making matters worse, Schnatter's comments were praised by white supremacists, and Papa John's responded by saying it did not want

4. Matt Bonesteel, "Papa John's Tried to Blame the NFL for Bad Sales," *Washington Post,* May 9, 2018, https://www.washingtonpost.com/news/early-lead/wp/2018/05/09/papa-johns-tried-to-blame-the-nfl-for-bad-sales-that-clearly-wasnt-the-issue/?noredirect=on&utm_term=.95e1518f5a16.

white supremacists or their groups buying its pizzas. Mr. Schnatter, an outsized figure at the company who appeared frequently in its commercials and owns 30% of its stock, stepped down as chief executive and resigned as chairman of the board in May 2018.[5]

Papa John's International, Inc. operates and franchises pizza delivery and carryout restaurants under the Papa John's trademark in the United States and internationally. It operates through five segments: Domestic Company-Owned Restaurants, North America Commissaries, North America Franchising, International Operations, and All Others. The company also operates dine-in and delivery restaurants. As of December 31, 2017, it operated 5,199 Papa John's restaurants, which included 743 company-owned and 4,456 franchised restaurants. The company was founded by John Schnatter in 1984 after selling his car and borrowing money to start his first pizza place.

In mid-January 2018, shares of Papa John traded at $68.62 per share. As turmoil swirled over the comments by Schnatter and his removal as president and resignation from the board, the share price dropped to $38.94 by August 8, 2018, a 43% drop in only seven months. With 31.62 million shares outstanding, the $29.68 per share drop in value equals a loss of $938 million.

LES MOONVES AND SEXUAL HARASSMENT CHARGES COST INVESTORS $2 BILLION. CBS Corporation operates as a mass media company worldwide. The company operates through four segments: Entertainment, Cable Networks, Publishing, and Local Media. The Entertainment segment distributes a schedule of news and public affairs broadcasts, and sports and entertainment programming; produces, acquires, and/or distributes programming, including series, specials, news, and public affairs; operates online content networks for information and entertainment; produces, acquires, and distributes theatrical motion pictures; and digital streaming services. The Cable Networks segment offers subscription program services, such as original series, theatrical feature films, documentaries, boxing and other sports-related programming, and special events. This segment also operates

5. Tiffany Hsu, "Racial Slur Leads to Papa John's Founder Quitting Chairman," *New York Times*, July 11, 2018, https://www.nytimes.com/2018/07/11/business/papa-johns-racial-slur.html.

CBS Sports Network, a 24-hour cable program service that provides college sports and related content; and Smithsonian Networks, which operates a channel featuring cultural, historical, scientific, and educational programs. The Publishing segment publishes and distributes adult and children's consumer books in printed, digital, and audio formats; develops special imprints and publishes titles based on the products of the company, as well as those of third parties; and distributes products for other publishers. This segment also delivers content; and promotes its products on its websites, social media, and general Internet sites, as well as those related to individual titles. The Local Media segment owns 29 broadcast television stations; and operates local websites, including content from the company's television stations. The company was founded in 1986 and is headquartered in New York, New York.

Les Moonves had a long career in the entertainment industry. At various points in his career he worked at 20th Century Fox Television, Lorimar Television, and Warner Bros. Television. He joined CBS in 1995 as president of CBS Entertainment. From April 1998 until 2003, he was president and chief executive officer at CBS Television, then was promoted to chairman and CEO of CBS in 2003. In 2003, CBS had 6 of the 10 most-watched primetime shows in the final quarter of 2005: *CSI, Without a Trace, CSI: Miami, Survivor: Guatemala, NCIS, and Cold Case*. He is also credited with the hugely successful *Everybody Loves Raymond*, and *The Big Bang Theory*. Moonves was a powerhouse in the entertainment industry.[6]

On Friday, July 24, 2018, *The New Yorker* published allegations about sexual misconduct by Les Moonves, CEO of CBS for the prior 24 years. The report detailed allegations of harassment by six women, some incidents occurring in the 1980s and 1990s.

On July 24, 2018, CBS stock traded at $57.53. The first day of trading after the *New Yorker* article was published about inappropriate behavior by Moonves, share prices of CBS began to fall and by July 30, 2018, share prices dropped to $51.28, a loss of $6.25 per share. With 338.52 million shares outstanding, the per share drop of $6.25 equaled a loss in shareholder value of $2.1 billion.

6. https://en.wikipedia.org/wiki/Les_Moonves.

STEVE WYNN AND SEXUAL HARASSMENT CHARGES COST INVESTORS $4 BILLION. In 1989, the grand opening of the Mirage Resort & Casino changed the Las Vegas Strip from glorified slot machine barns into a fabulous resort destination. The Mirage property was unprecedented in its size and upscale show offerings. This imaginative effort was the brainchild of Steve Wynn. In the prior history of Las Vegas, nothing like it had ever been seen before. From this exciting start, Steve Wynn built Wynn Resorts Ltd.

Wynn Resorts, Limited develops, owns, and operates destination casino resorts. As of February 15, 2018, the company's Wynn Macau segment had approximately 273,000 square feet of casino space, which offered 316 table games and 988 slot machines, private gaming salons, sky casinos, and a poker pit; 2 luxury hotel towers with a total of 1,008 guest rooms and suites; 8 food and beverage outlets; 59,000 square feet of retail space; 31,000 square feet of meeting and convention space; recreation and leisure facilities comprising 2 health clubs, spas, a salon, and a pool; and a rotunda show and a Chinese zodiac-inspired ceiling. Its Wynn Palace segment had approximately 420,000 square feet of casino space that offers 323 table games and 1,115 slot machines, private gaming salons, and sky casinos; a luxury hotel with a total of 1,706 guest rooms, suites, and villas; 11 food and beverage outlets; 106,000 square feet of retail space; 37,000 square feet of meeting and convention space; recreation and leisure facilities, including a gondola ride, health club, spa, salon, and pool; and public attractions, such as a performance lake and floral art displays.

The company's Las Vegas Operations segment had approximately 192,000 square feet of casino space, which provide 247 table games and 1,829 slot machines, private gaming salons, a sky casino, a poker room, and a race and sports book; 2 luxury hotel towers with a total of 4,748 guest rooms, suites, and villas; 33 food and beverage outlets; 110,000 square feet of retail space; 290,000 square feet of meeting and convention space; 3 nightclubs and a beach club; recreation and leisure facilities, including swimming pools, private cabanas, 2 full-service spas and salons, and a wedding chapel; and Le Rêve–The Dream, a water-based theatrical production and a theater presenting entertainment productions and various headliner entertainment acts. The company was founded in 2002 and is based in Las Vegas, Nevada.

At the beginning of January 2018, Wynn was a 75-year-old billionaire, chairman of Wynn Resorts and working on developing a $2.6 billion resort in Massachusetts. By the beginning of February, Wynn was unemployed. Wynn's sexual harassment story is special because he personally was Wynn Resorts and it was him. Once the story of sexual harassment broke, things went downhill real fast.

On January 26, 2018, the *Wall Street Journal* reported that there were accusations of sexual misconduct against Wynn over many decades. The next day, Wynn resigned as finance chair of the Republican National Committee. On January 30, 2018, The Nevada Gaming Control Board announced an investigation into Wynn's conduct. The regulatory authority can assess fines, revoke licenses, and halt commercial activity. On February 6, 2018, Wynn resigned as chairman and CEO of Wynn Resorts. He maintained he was innocent but said the torrent of negative publicity made it impossible for him to be effective. On February 7, 2018, a shareholder fund filed a lawsuit against the board of directors claiming they knew about sexual misconduct and failed to inform investors. This was quickly followed as three law firms began seeking investors in Wynn Resorts for a class action lawsuit against the board for its failure to report Wynn's alleged sexual misconduct. An insider trading action was launched by The New York State comptroller, acting on behalf of the New York State Common Retirement Fund, claiming that executives and five board members engaged in insider trading when they sold company stock while aware of the sexual misconduct allegations. On February 27, 2018, women in Las Vegas and Chicago prompted police departments to begin an investigation. One woman told police she felt coerced into a sexual relationship with Wynn in the 1970s. In March 2018, two massage therapists filed civil complaints against Wynn for intentional misconduct and alleged being coerced into having sex with Wynn. On March 7, 2018, two board members announced their plans to step down.[7]

On January 25, 2018 Wynn Resorts traded at $200.60. It dropped to $180.29 the next day and by January 29 dropped further hitting $163.47. The $37.13 per share drop in value is an 18.5% loss in just four days.

7. Khalon Richard, "After Sexual Misconduct Claims, Vegas Mogul Steve Wynn Fell Fast," *NPR*, March 15, 2018, https://www.npr.org/2018/03/15/592318034/after-sexual-misconduct-claims-vegas-mogul-steve-wynn-fell-fast.

The share price bounced around at the $160 level for a while and by mid-year recovered to its $200 level. After reaching back to the $200 level in mid-May the stock steadily fell and as of this writing in early September has dropped to $128.38. If the entire drop is credited to Wynn's behavior, then he caused investors a loss of 36% of shareholder value. If we only attribute the immediate 18.5% loss to the revelations about Wynn, the shareholder loss is huge. With 108.54 million shares outstanding, the $37.13 per share drop in value equals a loss of $4 billion.

HARVEY WEINSTEIN AND TOTAL LOSS. A lifetime of allegedly atrocious behavior led to the total loss of a very successful company. While not a public company, all those involved with the financial performance of the company have been wiped out.

In 2005, Harvey Weinstein co-founded the production-and-distribution companies Weinstein Company. It produced and distributed very successful independent films *Sex, Lies, and Videotape*, *The Crying Game*, *Pulp Fiction*, *The English Patient*, *Shakespeare in Love*, and *The King's Speech*. Weinstein's films have earned more than 300 Oscar nominations.

For more than 20 years, Weinstein has also been trailed by rumors of sexual harassment and assault but a variety of moves including legal threats and settlement payments have allegedly suppressed his history. On October 5, 2017, the *New York Times* reporters Jodi Kantor and Megan Twohey revealed multiple allegations of sexual harassment against Weinstein including unwanted touching, forced oral sex, and rape. The article led to the resignation of four members of the Weinstein Company and to Weinstein's firing. Allegations have swirled that executives and board members were aware of Weinstein's behavior (on October 10, the Weinstein Company's board issued a statement, writing that "these allegations come as an utter surprise to the Board. Any suggestion that the Board had knowledge of this conduct is false").[8]

The *New York Times* article spawned months of other investigative articles, and a New York City police investigation led to Harvey

8. Ronan Farrow, "From Aggressive Overtures to Sexual Assault: Harvey Weinstein's Accusers Tell Their Stories," *The New Yorker*, October 23, 2017, https://www.newyorker.com/news/news-desk/from-aggressive-overtures-to-sexual-assault-harvey-weinsteins-accusers-tell-their-stories.

Weinstein being charged with rape. Weinstein became repugnant and as his entity was closely tied to his company, Weinstein Company, was an outcast.

Victims of Weinstein, in a class action lawsuit, sued him and named his company as a co-defendant. Company employees, actresses, and models joined the lawsuit. A television production team sued the company over the collapse of a planned Amazon series, which was supposed to be produced by the firm but was scrapped after the scandal broke. The financial strain and unknowable outcome from the lawsuits drove Weinstein and Company into bankruptcy.

Weinstein Co. declared bankruptcy in March 2018 with less than $500,000 in cash after failing to find a buyer that would give the company a second life outside the protection of the court. Delaware bankruptcy judge Christopher Sontchi, at a hearing, signed off on the company's bankruptcy auction agreement to sell its assets to the Dallas-based private equity firm Lantern Capital Partners for $289 million.[9] All proceeds from the sales are expected to go to satisfy creditors and successful plaintiffs.

* * * *

It seems that well-behaved CEOs may not be able to justify their large compensation packages with correspondingly higher company performance, but when CEOs misbehave investors face risks and losses they never saw coming. The value of highly paid CEOs should be questioned when valuing a company's assembled workforce.

9. Ryan Faughnder, "Bankruptcy Judge Approves $21-Million Price Cut in Weinstein Co. Sale, Expected to Close Friday," *Los Angeles Times,* July11, 2018, http://www.latimes.com/business/hollywood/la-fi-ct-weinstein-co-lantern-20180711-story.html#.

CHAPTER **16A**

ROYALTY RATES FOR LICENSING, DATA SOURCES

The following sources for royalty rate data are described in this new chapter.

***Royalty Rates for Technology*, seventh edition**, represents over a decade of research. You will find information about technology royalty rates, license fees, milestone payments, and much more—all from real deals between independent parties. Also reported is information about infringement damage awards and settlements. Each data item describes the technology, identifies the parties involved in the deal and shows the financial terms. All of the information in this book is provided to show different types of value indications for various technologies in different industries and is the most comprehensive book of its kind on the market. Industries covered in this report include:

Technology	Page
Rubber Recycling—Common stock plus 3% sales	584
Tire Recycling— 5% on sales	585
Tire Recycling—2% on sales	585
Tire Recycling—$1 million license fee plus $4 per ton of processed tires	586
Tire Incinerator—Cash, common stock and 2% of sales	586
Toxic Recycling—$525,000 plus 3% of sales	587
Toxic Waste Furnaces—Common stock and 2% of sales	588
Waste to Energy Conversion—$10 million	589
Waste to Oil—$100,000 plus 10% of sales	590
Waste Water Treatment—Common stock and 2% of sales	590
Visit www.ipresearh.com.	

***Royalty Rates for Trademarks & Copyrights*, fifth edition** provides a readily accessible guide to royalty rate information for trademarks and copyrights based on real-world transactions. Each data item describes the subject trademark or copyright, identifies the parties involved in the deal, and shows the financial terms. Also reported are other indications of value derived from details of recent acquisitions. The information in this book has been collected from reliable sources since September 1990 and is considered to represent a comprehensive collection of trademark and copyright pricing information. Only reputable sources of information have been used. These include filings with the Security & Exchange Commission, company press releases, and court opinions. Some of the information comes from highly respected newspapers. The information contained this book is organized by industry as follows: Airline, Apparel, Architecture, Art, Automotive, Beverages, Celebrities, Communications, Corporate Names, Electronics, Food, Franchises, Furniture, General Merchandise, Hotels, Internet, Media, Medical, Movies, Music, Party Goods, Personnel Care, Publishing, Restaurants, Services, Sports, Toys, and University Names. Visit www.ipresearh.com.

***Royalty Rates for Pharmaceuticals & Biotechnology*, eighth edition** contains an enormous amount of information about drug therapy technology pricing. Each data item describes the subject drug technology, identifies the parties involved in the deal and shows the financial terms. Only reputable sources of information have been used. These include filings with the Security & Exchange Commission., company press releases, and court opinions. Some of the information comes from highly respected newspapers. This book represents over a decade of research. Included in these pages you will find information about royalty rates, license fees, and milestone payments for the following technologies:

Agriculture—Animal Health
Agriculture—Golden Rice
Alcohol Dependency Treatment
Alpha Interferon—Natural
Alzheimer's Diagnostic Test
Alzheimer's Treatment
Anesthetic
Animal Health Products
Anti-hypertension Therapy
Anti-infection Screening Process
Anti-inflammatory Drug BB-882
Anti-inflammatory—Topical
Antifungal Agent—Amphotericin B
Anti-viral Therapy
Anti-viral and Anti-infective Therapies
Arginine Products
Arthritis—Rheumatoid—Drug Humira
Asthma Drug—Oral Administration
Attention Deficit Hyperactivity Disorder
Blood Cell Therapy
Blood Clot Formation Test
Blood Expander
Blood—Hematology Controls
Blood Plasma Volume Expander
BPI—Human Protein
Cancer Treatments
Cardiovascular Treatments
Cartilage Regenerative Technology
Catheter Technology

Cell Adhesion Technology
Cell Cultures
Chimeric IgG1 antibodies
Chromosome Analysis Technology
Chronic Pulmonary Disease Therapy
Cold Remedies
Collagenase Ointment
Consensus Interferon
Contraceptives
Contrast Agent—Intravenous
Cough Medicine
Cyclin-Dependent Kinasc Assay Test Kit
Cypress Stem Cells
Cystic Fibrosis Treatment
Cytomegalovirus Intravenous Treatment
Dermatology
Diabetes
Diagnostic Imagining Using Ligands
Dietary Supplement—Botanical
Diltiazem Heart Drug
DNA Binding Invention
Drug Delivery
EGF Fusion Protein
Enoxaparin
Environmental Test Kit
Enzyme Inhibitors
Epilepsy Treatment
EPO, Hepatitis B, and IL-2
Estrogen Replacement Therapy
Fibrotic Disease Therapy
Financing Research
Gene Activation Technology
Gene Alteration Technology
Genetic Abnormalities Test– Prenatal
Gene Splicing Technology
Genetically Engineered Listeria Therapy
Genetic Research

Gene Sequencing
Gene Therapy Partnership Network
Genetic Technology
Genomics-Based Drug Discovery
Hepatitis
Hepatitis A
Hepatitis A Vaccine
Hepatitis B
Hepatitis B & C Treatment
Hepatitis C
Hepatitis C protease Inhibitor
Hepatitis E Vaccine
HIV
Human Growth Hormone
Human Monoclonal Antibodies Technology
Humanization Antibody
Humanized Antibody
Humanized Monoclonal Antibody
Hypertension Treatment
Hypertension Treatment—Autologous Gene Therapy
Immune (idiopathic) Thrombocytopenic Purpura Therapy
Immune System Regulators—Cytokines
Immunodeficiency
Immunotoxin—MDX-RA
Inflammation Antibody-based Therapeutics
Inflammatory—Topical Therapy
Influenza Drug
Insomnia
Insomnia Therapy
Integrelin Drug
Interferon Gamma-1b
Interferon—Natural
Intracellular Receptor Technology
Kidney Disease Treatment
Kidney Failure Treatment
Living Cells Connective Tissue
Mammary Cell Growth Inhibitor

Microorganism Detection in Water
Microsponge Delivery System
Migraine Relief
Modulation of Opioid Receptors
Monoclonal Antibody Technology
Multiple Sclerosis
Multiple Sclerosis Therapy
Naked DNA Technology
Nanocrystalline Particles
NASA Technology
Nasal Vitamin B-12 Therapy
Natural Cell Signaling Phenomenon
Nerve Repair
Nervous System Therapeutics
NeuroCell Joint Venture
Neurodegenerative and Psychiatric Therapy
Neurological
Neurological Peptide Therapy
Neurological Therapeutics
Neurotrophic Factor Commercialization
Nuclear Matrix Protein Technology
Nucleic Acid Probe Technology
Nucleic Acid Sequences for Detection
Nucleic Acid Targeting
Nucleic Acid Technologies
Neurological Disorders
Neurological Disorders Anti-agitation Drug
Nicotine Addiction Treatment
Nutrition—Salt Alternative
Obesity Therapy
Ophthalmic
Oral Contraceptive
Osteoporosis Compound
Oxygenation
Pain Management Therapies
Personal Care Products
Photodynamic Therapy

Polymerase Chain Reaction Technology
ADP Ribose Polymerase Diagnostic Assay
Pre-eclampsia/Toxemia Diagnosis Therapy
Pro-Apolipoprotein A-I and Lipid Complexes
Progesterone Gel
Protein Secretion Technology
Proteomics Technology
Psychiatric and Psychotic Therapy
Psychotherapeutic Drugs
Pulmonary Disease
Rapid Diagnostic Test
RAS Human Protein/Rational Drug Design
Recombinant Human Erythropoietin- Procrit®
Recombinant Technology
Respiratory Therapy
Rhenium Radiotherapy and Monoclonal Antibodies
Ribozymes
RNAi Interference Technology
RNAi Interference Therapies
Sarafem®
Schizophrenia
Schizophrenia and Bipolar Treatment
Septic Shock Treatment
Sexual Dysfunction Therapy
Skin Technology
Sleep Therapy—Nasal Administration
Spirulina
Spleen Tyrosine Kinase Inhibitor
Stem Cells
Stem Cell Proliferation Factor
Stem Cell Technology and Materials
Stem Cells—Pluripotent Novel Strains
Stem-loop Vector Technology
Stromal Derived Factor 1 (SDF-1) Peptide Agonists and Antagonists
Tamiflu™
Thalidomide
Thalidomide Analogs

Tissue Malignancy Treatments
Thymidine Kinase Isoenzyme Diagnostics
Transdermal Estrogen Patch
Tropical Plants
Ultrasound Contrast Agent
Vaccines, gene-based
Vaccine Research
Virus Vaccines
Wart Removal Products
Water-Jel Sterile Burn Dressings
Yeast-based Screening Technology

Visit www.ipresearh.com.

Royalty Rates for Medical Devices & Diagnostics 2016 is all about royalty rates from the medical device industry. It is based on decades of research. The rates in this book can be used for negotiating licenses, valuing medical technology, and establishing patent infringement damages. Each data item describes the subject drug technology, identifies the parties involved in the deal, and shows the financial terms. Only reputable sources of information have been used. These include filings with the Security & Exchange Commission, company press releases, and court opinions. Some of the information comes from highly respected newspapers. Included in these pages you will find information about royalty rates, license fees, and milestone payments for:

Technology	Page
Polymer—Biomedical	110
Prostate Treatment	110
Radiation Therapy	111
Radiation Therapy Breathing Motion Management	112
Skin Barrier Repair	112
Skin Care	113
Skin Care	113
Skin Treatment	113
Spinal Implants	113
Spinal Implants	114
Spinal Implants	114
Syringe Disposal	115
Syringe	115
Syringe	115
Safety Syringe	116
Surgical Device	116
Surgical Device	117
Surgical Device	117
Surgical Procedure	118
Tissue Growth and Repair	119
Transcatheter Valve Technology	120
Vascular Closure Device	120
Vascular Closure Device	121
Vascular Closure Device	121
Voiding Dysfunction Therapy	122
Wound Closure	123
X-Ray Product	124
Visit www.ipresearh.com.	

RoyaltySource® has been tracking intellectual property news and licenses related to technology (patent, know-how, trade secret, and business method), software, trademark, trade name, brand or logo, copyright and right of publicity for 30 years. In addition, they also collect franchise agreements as well as fee agreements, such as agency/representation, commission sales, consultant, and services agreements.

The company applies a two-tier screening process to ensure the most comprehensive database of royalty payments, without the inclusion of irrelevant records. Using proprietary technology, RoyaltySource's IT specialists pre-screen the massive amount of information, selecting only those transactions containing royalty rates (%). The second tier is performed by intellectual property experts. They check record by record to assure that RoyaltySource's clients receive comprehensive and relevant data.

Clients use RoyaltySource reports for several purposes, including license agreement negotiation, valuation, litigation, infringement damage measurement, and transfer pricing.

RoyaltySource will forward customers a login to access a summarized list of records based on a customer's requests. The preliminary report is created for customers that call-in with a specific request, thereby receiving a customized experience and saving an enormous amount of time. Customers select and pay for only those data items that are relevant to their needs. Once selections are made, RoyaltySource delivers a final report with all selected records, featuring an abstract page detailing:

- Royalty rates as a percentage of some financial bottom line
- Licensee and Licensor information
- Description of the property licensed or sold, such as IP Property, Field of Use
- Other compensation, such as milestone and upfront payments
- Transaction terms, such as agreement date, exclusivity, geographical restrictions
- Arm's length or related party status as available
- Source of information (SEC filings, news articles, company news releases)
- Visit RoyaltySource at http://royaltysource.com.

RoyaltyStat® is a reliable source of royalty rates extracted from unredacted license agreements. RoyaltyStat's rates are used in transfer pricing, purchase price allocation, intellectual property valuation, and due diligence connected with litigation, business development, bankruptcy, and mergers and acquisitions. RoyaltyStat provides curated data and custom-built tools to determine arm's length royalty rates and profit indicators specified in the OECD Transfer Pricing Guidelines and the United Nations Practical Manual on Transfer Pricing for Developing Countries. Counting over 18 years of online experience, RoyaltyStat's reliable data extraction helps clients support tax audit, planning, and contemporaneous documentation. RoyaltyStat serves corporations, government agencies, accounting, consulting, and law firms with their databases and consulting services. RoyaltyStat is a subscription-based service. Visit: https://www.royaltystat.com/.

Royalty Range is a database provider with three professional databases, covering royalty rates, loan interest rates, and service fees. Its third-party comparables data is used for a number of purposes, including transfer pricing financial transaction benchmarking, royalty rates and service fees benchmarking, valuation of intangibles, and purchase price allocations. Multinational enterprises, global consulting companies, international law firms, and government authorities in more than 60 countries use their databases to access data quickly and easily.

Royalty Range has locations in the United States, the UK, and Belgium. Royalty Range is funded by the European Union's Structural Funds, with a total share capital of USD $1,000,000.

The Royalty Range database has been featured in publications by the Organisation for Economic Co-operation and Development (OECD), the World Bank Group (WBG), the International Monetary Fund (IMF), and the United Nations (UN).

Key aspects of Royalty Range are:

- Its data is fully compliant with the OECD base erosion and profit-shifting (BEPS) requirements and U.S, regulations.
- Each agreement is manually analyzed for up to 50 comparability factors.
- The databases include detailed functional, risk, cost, and asset analyses.
- Customers receive detailed, manually prepared summaries of the agreement terms and comparability factors.
- The data is fully analyzed, clean, structured, and manually prepared for each agreement.

- Royalty Range does not include duplicates, redacted agreements, undisclosed remuneration terms, or remuneration types other than percentages.
- Parties to the agreements are checked for independence.
- All information is provided in Excel or Word, together with links to original sources and PDF documents.
- The data is continually improving through constant usage, double-checking, and new information.
- An easy-to-perform analysis can be completed in a matter of hours by accepting or rejecting agreements that have already been analyzed, and double-checking them for quality.
- Visit: Royaltyrange.com

Marketables® provides data that relate trademark to its revenues, to profits, and to other assets of the business. This services is all about trademarks.

Marketables data contains the results of 10,303 trademark valuations and 6,638 customer valuations published in the financial reports of over 15,000 listed companies from all over the world. These valuations stem from purchase price allocations, impairment tests, trademark deals, intragroup royalty payments, and from other occasions. Each record contains trademark value, revenues, reported or implied trademark royalty rates, customer value, enterprise value, trademark profit split, and other data, and a detailed description of the business as of the date of the valuation. All trademark values and royalty rates are audited and/or conforming to accepted accounting standards, that is, fair value, market price, or arm's length. A few records, containing only partial information, are charged at half price. Data allow the benchmarking and comparison of most meaningful valuation ratios and multiples. Cases are truly global from over 100 countries and most up-to-date, with 60% of entries from the last 5 years. Regular updates with approximately 1,000 new entries per year. Visit: www.marketables.net.

CHAPTER **27A**

EXMARK ESTABLISHES NEW ROYALTY DAMAGES MODEL

In *Exmark Manufacturing Company v. Briggs & Stratton Power*,[1] the U.S. Court of Appeals for the Federal Circuit approved a reasonable royalty damages theory based on the total value of an accused product, even though the patented invention was only part of a multicomponent product.

In Chapter 27, page 272 of the main text, the Entire Market Value (EMV) Rule is explained as follows.

"The 'entire market value rule' recognizes that the economic value of a patent may be greater than the value of the sales of the patented part alone. Under this rule, courts have allowed recovery of lost profits or a reasonable royalty based not only on the profit from the patented part, but also on non-patented parts."[2] The entire market value rule "permits recovery of damages based on the value of the entire apparatus containing several features, where the patent related feature is the basis for customer demand."[3] The entire market value rule has come under attack and in some cases is far too limiting and results in inadequate damages awards.

---

1. *Exmark Manufacturing Co., Inc. v. Briggs & Stratton Power Group, LLC*, No. 16-2197 (Fed. Cir. 2018).
2. *King Instruments Corp. v. Perego*, 65 F.3d 941, 950–951 n.4 (Fed. Cir.1986).
3. *State Indus., Inc. v. Mor-Flo Indus.*, Inc., 883 F.2d 1573, 1580 (Fed. Cir. 1989).

In *Mentor Graphics Corp. v. EVE-USA Inc.*[4] the concept of the entire market rule was an issue. A jury awarded Mentor over $36 million in lost products based on the patent-infringing sales of the defendant's product that were made for Intel Corp. The defendant appealed the decision arguing that the court failed to properly apportion the lost profits. They argued that the damages amount must be apportioned to cover only the portion of the profit attributable to the infringing products patented feature.

The Patent Act provides: "the court shall award [the patent owner] damages adequate to compensate for the infringement but in no event less than a reasonable royalty for the use made of the invention by the infringer."[5] Under the statute, "damages adequate to compensate" means "full compensation for any 'any damages' [the patent owner] suffered as a result of the infringement."

The Federal Circuit considered the four *Panduit* factors and concluded that Mentor satisfied all four and was entitled to an award based on lost profits. The Federal Circuit rejected the argument of the defendant and reasoned that Mentor's product and the defendants' infringing product were the only acceptable alternatives to Intel and Intel would not purchase a product without the patented features. The court considered that other features of the product may have been important to Intel but only Mentor could sell the product with all the desired features including the patented feature at issue. The Federal Circuit concluded that but for the infringing products, Mentor would have made sales and profits based on the entire market value of the product sales it had lost—no apportionment was justified.

The EMV rule is also applicable to damages based on a reasonable royalty, which is typically divided into two components: (1) the determination of the royalty base and (2) the determination of the royalty rate. For example, the royalty base could be the net sales in dollars of the allegedly infringing product, and the royalty rate could be a running royalty expressed as a percent of the sales price of the product. The reasonable royalty damages calculation is then expressed as the product of the royalty base multiplied by the royalty rate.

4. No. 15-1470 (Fed. Cir. Mar.16, 2017).
5. 35 U.S.C. § 284.

Chisum[6] divides the EMV rule into two categories: (1) apportionment and (2) complementary products. *Apportionment* refers to instances where the patented invention is part of a larger product. Chisum cites *Bose Corp.*[7] for guidance when applying the EMV rule, namely that the patent-related feature must be the basis for customer demand where the court stated that "the '721 patent improved the performance of the loudspeakers and contributed substantially to the increased demand for products in which it was incorporated."

Complementary products refer to instances where another physically separate product is sold with the patented invention. Chisum cites *Rite-Hite Corporation v. Kelley*[8] for guidance in applying the EMV rule, namely that the physically separate products function together in some manner to produce a desired end result and not simply as a matter of convenience or business advantage. In *Rite-Hite* the court stated: "Although the two devices may have been used together, they did not function together to achieve one result and each could effectively have been used independently of each other. . . ." When applying the EMV rule, Chisum does not identify or imply that there are any differences or distinctions between the two categories with respect to the role that the patented feature plays in the demand for the overall product or products as well as the applicability of the rule to the royalty rate or the royalty base.

EMV AND REASONABLE ROYALTY DAMAGES

Much of the recent attention and case law related to the potential use or misuse of the EMV rule focuses on the royalty base. Damages are determined by focusing on the portion of the infringing product that directly uses the infringed technology. Once this portion is identified it becomes the royalty base to which a reasonable royalty rate is applied to determine damages. The apportionment effort has become known as identifying the *smallest saleable unit* of the overall infringing product using the infringed

6. Donald S. Chisum, Craig Allen Nard, Herbert F. Schwartz, Pauline Newman and F. Scott Kieff, *Principles of Patent Law: Cases and Materials*, 3rd ed. (New York: Foundation Press, 2004), 10: 1329–1330.

7. *Bose Corp. v. JBL, Inc.*, 274 F.3d 1354, 1361 (Fed. Cir. 2001).

8. *Rite-Hite Corporation v. Kelley.*

technology. This might be an actual part associated with the infringing product or sometimes a hypothetically defined portion of a product.

The determination of damages in the form of a reasonable royalty is case- and fact-specific, and there is no a priori reason why the EMV rule should be applied only to the base or that the base should be the more appropriate place to apply the EMV rule than the rate. Nonetheless, the majority of cases rely on identifying a royalty base that reflects the specific contribution of an infringed patented technology. There is no reason why reversal of this norm would not provide a satisfactory damages calculation where the base is the entire value of the infringing product and the rate reflects the apportionment for capturing the economic contribution of the infringed technology. Recently, in *Exmark Manufacturing Company v. Briggs & Stratton Power*, the U.S. Court of Appeals for the Federal Circuit approved a reasonable royalty damages theory where apportionment is captured by the royalty rate.[9]

EXMARK MANUFACTURING COMPANY V. BRIGGS & STRATTON POWER

Exmark Manufacturing Company filed suit against Briggs & Stratton Power Products Group, LLC in the United States District Court for the District of Nebraska, alleging infringement of, inter alia, claim 1 of U.S. Patent No. 5,987,863. The district court entered summary judgment that claim 1 was not invalid because the claim survived multiple reexaminations involving the same prior art. The district court also denied summary judgment of indefiniteness with respect to claim 1. The case proceeded to a jury trial, where the jury found that Briggs willfully infringed Exmark's patent. The jury awarded $24,280,330 in compensatory damages, which the district court doubled as enhanced damages for Briggs' willful infringement.

Briggs appealed several of the district court's orders, including the district court's (1) summary judgment that claim 1 is not anticipated or obvious, (2) denial of summary judgment that claim 1 is indefinite, (3) denial of a new trial on damages, (4) evidentiary rulings related to damages, (5) denial of a new trial on willfulness, and (6) denial of Briggs's laches defense.

9. The information discussed in this new chapter is from the website for the United States Court of Appeals for the Federal Circuit, *Exmark Manufacturing Company v. Briggs & Stratton Power* [Opinion], http://www.cafc.uscourts.gov/node/22840.

The court concluded the district court erred by basing its summary judgment of no invalidity solely on the fact that claim 1 survived multiple reexaminations and vacated the district court's summary judgment of no invalidity.

The court also held that the district court erred in denying a new trial on damages because Exmark's damages expert failed to provide an adequate explanation as to how she arrived at a 5% royalty rate for the patented feature relative to other conventional features of the accused products.

The court also concluded that the district court abused its discretion by limiting the evidence relevant to damages to prior art that had been commercialized.

Additionally the court concluded that the district court abused its discretion by excluding from the willfulness trial evidence relating to patent validity based on its determination that Briggs's invalidity defenses were objectively unreasonable and vacated the jury's finding of willfulness, vacated the jury's damages award, vacated the district court's enhanced damages award.

The court also affirmed the district court's denial of summary judgment that claim 1 is indefinite, and affirmed its denial of Briggs's laches defense.

Exmark did not come out all that well in most areas of the appeal, including damages, but a new royalty damages model came out of the ruling. The remainder of this new chapter will focus on the court's opinion as it relates to damages, but first some background information will be useful.

EXMARK V. BRIGGS & STRATTON BACKGROUND

Briggs and Exmark are competitors in the high-end commercial lawn mower industry. Exmark filed suit against Briggs and Schiller Grounds Care, Inc., alleging, inter alia, infringement of claim 1 of the '863 patent. The '863 patent is directed to a lawn mower having improved flow control baffles. A baffle is a metal structure under the mower deck that directs air flow and grass clippings during operation.

Claim 1 requires a side wall discharge opening and a "first flow control baffle" having a certain shape. Specifically, the claim recites that the first baffle comprises "a first arcuate baffle portion," "a first elongated and substantially straight baffle portion," and "a second arcuate baffle portion," with the elongated and substantially straight baffle portion "angularly disposed . . . in a chord-like fashion" with respect to the second cutting blade.[10] The parties refer to this as a "curved-straight-curved" baffle.

On appeal, Briggs provides an annotated version of the '863 patent depicting the claimed curved-straight-curved baffle.

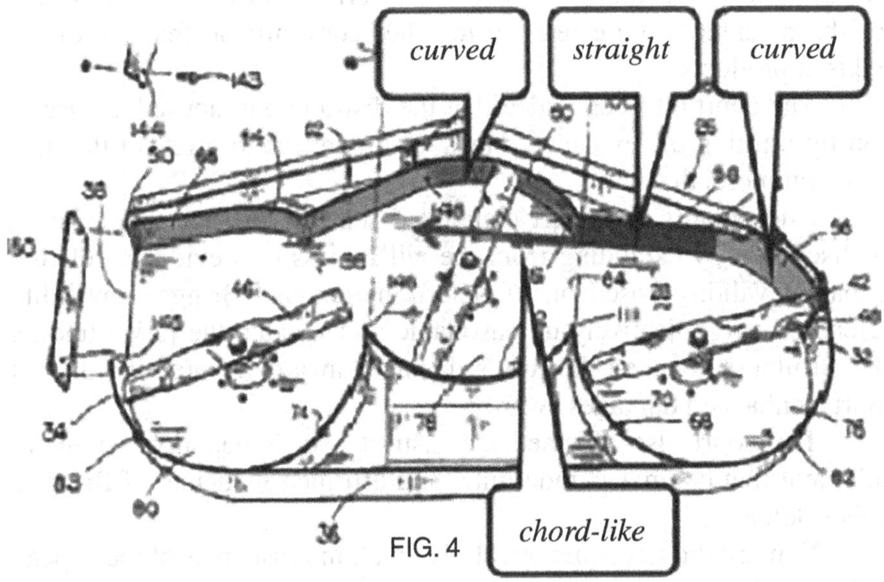

Exmark's patent was directed to an improved flow control baffle for a lawn mower that efficiently guides glass clippings from under the lawn mower and out of a side chute. The asserted patent claim was directed to a "multiblade lawn mower" as a whole, comprising the innovative flow control baffle component along with other traditional lawn mower elements.

DAMAGES

Briggs presented three specific arguments on appeal.

First, Briggs asserted that the district court erred by permitting Exmark to use the sales price of the accused mowers as the royalty base instead of the sales price of the flow control baffles.

10. US Patent No. 5,987,863 at col. 6 ll. 21–39.

Second, Briggs argued that Exmark's damages expert's opinion should have been excluded because she failed to adequately explain how she arrived at her proposed 5% royalty rate.

Finally, Briggs asserted that the district court improperly excluded evidence relevant to damages.

ENTIRE MARKET VALUE ACCEPTED AS THE ROYALTY BASE. Briggs argued that the district court erred by allowing Exmark to compute a royalty rate without properly identifying a royalty base to apportion the value of the patentee's invention in comparison to the value of the whole lawn mower. The parties did not dispute that apportionment is required in this case.

The court recognized that a reasonable royalty award must be based on the incremental value that the patented invention adds to the end product. In this case, the patent makes clear that the patented improvement relates to the mower's flow control baffle, which through its structure and orientation within the mower deck purportedly efficiently directs grass clippings toward a side-discharge and thereby improves the quality of grass cut in a manner that distinguishes it from prior art.

The remaining limitations of claim 1 recite conventional features of a lawn mower, including a mower deck, a side-discharge opening, and a power means for operating the mower. The court agreed that in these circumstances, the patent owner must apportion or separate the damages between the patented improvement and the conventional components of the multicomponent product. This ensures that Exmark is compensated for the patented improvement (i.e., the improved flow control baffle) rather than the entire mower.

Briggs argued that Exmark's expert should have apportioned or separated the value of the baffle from the other features of the mower through the royalty base rather than the royalty rate. The court agreed.

The court affirmed that apportionment can be addressed in a variety of ways, including by careful selection of the royalty base to reflect the value added by the patented feature or by adjustment of the royalty rate so as to discount the value of a product's non-patented features; or by a combination thereof.

The court held that so long as Exmark adequately and reliably apportions between the improved and conventional features of the accused mower, using the accused mower as a royalty base and apportioning through the royalty rate is an acceptable methodology.

Using the accused lawn mower sales as the royalty base is particularly appropriate in this case because the asserted claim is, in fact, directed to the lawn mower as a whole. The preamble of claim 1 recites a "multiblade lawn mower."[11] It is not the baffle that infringes the claim, but rather the entire accused mower. Thus, claim 1 covers the infringing product as a whole, not as a single component of a multi-component product. There is no unpatented or non-infringing feature of the product. Nonetheless, "[w]hen a patent covers the infringing product as a whole, and the claims recite both conventional elements and unconventional elements, the court must determine how to account for the relative value of the patentee's invention in comparison to the value of the conventional elements recited in the claim, standing alone."[12] AstraZeneca AB v. Apotex Corp., 782 F.3d 1324, 1338 (Fed. Cir. 2015) (citing Ericsson, 773 F.3d at 1233).

The court noted that Exmark's use of the accused lawn mower sales as the royalty base is consistent with the realities of a hypothetical negotiation and accurately reflects the real-world bargaining that occurs, particularly in licensing. As we stated in *Lucent Technologies, Inc. v. Gateway, Inc.*, "the hypothetical negotiation tries, as best as possible, to recreate the ex ante licensing negotiation scenario and to describe the resulting agreement."[13]

The court stated that they understood that parties "routinely enter into license agreements that base the value of the patented inventions as a percentage of the commercial products' sales price," and thus "there is nothing inherently wrong with using the market value of the entire product, especially when there is no established market value for the infringing component or feature, so long as the multiplier (royalty rate) accounts for the proportion of the base represented by the infringing

11. US Patent No. 5,987,863 patent col. 5 l. 60.

12. *AstraZeneca AB v. Apotex Corp.*, 782 F.3d 1324, 1338 (Fed. Cir. 2015) (citing *Ericsson*, 773 F.3d at 1233).

13. 580 F.3d 1301, 1325 (Fed. Cir. 2009).

component or feature." This is consistent with the settlement agreement relied on by Exmark's damages expert, which the parties agree provided an effective royalty of 3.64% of the sales of the accused mowers.

The court upheld the use of the entire price of the mower as the royalty base for calculating reasonable royalty damages and established a new method for calculating damages. But the court rejected Exmark's damages expert's opinion because it failed to adequately tie the expert's proposed reasonable royalty rate to the facts of this case. Reviewing the court's problems with the other elements of the damages opinion is worthwhile.

REJECTION OF DAMAGES EXPERT'S OPINION. The court stated, "After a discussion of each of the *Georgia-Pacific* factors, including the benefits of the patented technology, sales and profitability, and the competitive relationship of the parties, Exmark's expert concluded with little explanation that Exmark and Briggs would have agreed to a 5% reasonable royalty rate on the sales of the accused lawn mowers as the value for the improved baffle."

The court complained that Exmark's expert did not tie the relevant *Georgia-Pacific* factors to the 5% royalty rate or explain how she calculated a 5% royalty rate using these factors.

Exmark's expert began her analysis by explaining her understanding of the benefits of the mowers covered by the '863 patent. Relying on the testimony of experts and fact witnesses, she identified a number of advantages arising from the use of the claimed baffle, including improved air and grass flow for reduced blowout, in-creased grass cut quality, minimized grass clumping, and more uniform discharge, all of which improve the mower's function and allows a mower to go faster in heavy grass areas. She concluded that negotiators would have recognized the importance of these advantages to customers and operators and the key role they play in Briggs's sale of its mowers. She repeated these advantages as relevant to *Georgia-Pacific* factors nine (utility and advantage of the patented technology) and ten (the nature of the patented invention). But she did not explain how these advantages, or her analysis of the *Georgia-Pacific* factors, led to her proposed 5% royalty rate. She addressed the two *Georgia-Pacific* factors but did not explain how they supported a 5% royalty rate.

When an expert employs the *Georgia-Pacific* factors, "reciting each factor and making a conclusory remark about its impact on the damages calculation before moving on does no more than tell the jury what factors a damages analysis could take into consideration."[14]

The court wanted more than a recitation of the *Georgia-Pacific* factors. When performing a *Georgia-Pacific* analysis, damages experts must not only analyze the applicable factors, but also carefully tie those factors to the proposed royalty rate.

It was not enough for Exmark's expert to explain the advantages of the baffle claimed in the '863 patent and state that they would have been important in a hypothetical negotiation. This told the jury nothing more than that the patented technology was important and commercially successful. A reasonable royalty analysis requires that "the trial court . . . carefully tie proof of damages to the claimed invention's footprint in the market place."[15] ResQNet.com, Inc. v. Lansa, Inc., 594 F.3d 860, 869 (Fed. Cir. 2010). To sufficiently tie the advantages of the patented baffles to the royalty rate in this case, Exmark's expert was required to explain the extent to which they factored into the value of the lawn mower and her 5% royalty rate.

Georgia-Pacific factor thirteen requires consideration of "the portion of realized profits attributable to non-patented elements". Exmark's expert acknowledged that other elements of the mowers affect sales and profits of the mowers, including durability, reliability, brand position, dealer support, and warranty. The court said the expert failed to conduct any analysis indicating the degree to which these considerations impact the market value or profitability of the mower and therefore impacted her suggested 5% royalty rate.

The expert acknowledged that Briggs and its co-defendant, Schiller, have patents covering other components of the accused mowers. But she ignored those components, opining without support that they do not relate to the quality of cut, which she considered "paramount" to selling mowers. Merely concluding that other components do not affect the value of the accused mower amounts to nothing more than speculation.

14. *Whitserve, LLC v. Computer Packages, Inc.*, 694 F.3d 10, 31 (2012).
15. *ResQNet.com, Inc. v. Lansa, Inc.*, 594 F.3d 860, 869 (Fed. Cir. 2010).

This problem might have been addressed with evidence itemizing the relative value of these other components. This might have improved the jury's understanding of the value of the baffle in relation to the other components of the accused multi-component mower.

The court stated that, "the remainder of Exmark's expert's opinion similarly recited the remaining *Georgia-Pacific* factors and either stated that they did not apply or provided a cursory explanation of the evidence considered for each factor. The opinion is devoid of any analysis tying either the evidence or the specific *Georgia-Pacific* factors to the proposed 5% royalty rate."

Exmark defends its expert's opinion, arguing she relied on quantitative market valuation evidence in forming her opinion. Exmark further stated that she considered evidence such as Briggs' selling value documents, detailing the value that Briggs placed on each of its mower's components, a litigation settlement agreement involving the '863 patent resulting in a comparable effective royalty rate, and the parties' profit margins during the damages period. The court recognized that Exmark's expert discussed quantitative market evidence in her opinion but found it troublesome that even assuming she properly considered this evidence, she failed to explain how the evidence factored into the proposed royalty rate. The court concluded that Exmark's expert merely addressed the *Georgia-Pacific* factors in light of the facts and then plucked the 5% royalty rate out of nowhere. Briggs next challenged three of the district court's evidentiary rulings related to damages.

Briggs first argued that the district court improperly excluded evidence of certain prior art, which it argued was related to the damages analysis. Specifically, Briggs sought to present evidence of conventional modes of mowing to rebut Exmark's argument that the mower claimed in the '863 patent was a big advancement over the prior art. Briggs argued that by showing the jury the small differences between the invention and prior art mowers, it would have demonstrated that many of the benefits Exmark attributed to the baffle were already present in the prior art. The district court allowed the introduction of some prior art but excluded any prior art that had not been commercialized, holding that "prior art is relevant to damages only to the extent that the patent was used in a product."[16] The district court appears to have based its ruling on the language of *Georgia-Pacific* factor nine, which considers "old modes or devices, if any, that had been used for working out similar results."[17]

PRIOR ART AS DAMAGES EVIDENCE. The court concluded that the district court abused its discretion by holding that prior art is relevant to damages only to the extent that the prior art was commercialized. Neither the district court nor Exmark cited any case to support the view that *Georgia-Pacific* factor nine limits evidence of prior art to commercialized modes or devices. The court also did not see any reason for such a narrow reading.

The fact that some prior art mowers were not commercialized does not make them immaterial to determining the extent to which the mower claimed in the '863 patent provides utility and advantages over the prior art.

The district court also limited the damages evidence to prior art directed to side-discharge mowers. The record demonstrates that commercial lawn mowers come in two varieties, mulching mowers and side-discharge mowers. Briggs argued that the district court abused its discretion by excluding prior art directed to mulching mowers. The court disagreed. The only asserted claim of the '863 patent requires a side-discharge mower. Therefore, it was reasonable and within the district court's discretion to exclude prior art mowers that were not side-discharge mowers.

Briggs also argued the district court abused its discretion by excluding evidence of Exmark's purportedly delayed decision to sue for infringement. Briggs argues that such delay undermines Exmark's evidence that it would never have condoned infringement without a high royalty.

The court agreed with the district court that Briggs's attempt to introduce evidence of Exmark's delay in filing suit for infringement is not relevant to damages, even when considering *Georgia-Pacific* factors four (licensing policy) and fifteen (hypothetical negotiation).

16. *Exmark Mfg. Co. v. Briggs & Stratton Power Prods. Grp., LLC*, No. 8:10:CV187, 2015 WL 5177759, at *4 (D. Neb. Sept. 4, 2015).

17. *Georgia-Pacific*, 318 F. Supp. at 1120 (emphasis added).

As the district court recognized, "The argument that the delay in bringing suit somehow establishes Exmark's perception of the value of its invention is specious. There are many reasons to forego filing a lawsuit, to imply that Exmark did so because it did not think the invention had value is speculative."

Brigg's appeal regarding Exmark's damages expert was generally a victory. More importantly, those performing damages calculations have been provided with support to accomplishing apportionment that focuses on the entire value of the infringing product as the royalty base.

APPENDIX C1

FOOD & BEVERAGE INDUSTRY ROYALTY RATES AND SUPPORT FROM THE 25% RULE

Food and beverage companies abound, and store shelves are crowded with a huge selection of competitive products. Populations of developed nations around the world are experiencing slow growth. The opportunities for food and beverage companies are reduced to capturing market share from other industry players. Product pricing is squeezed, and profit margins are growing ever thinner. The top 25 food and beverage companies in the United States have continued to lose market share, averaging annual sales growth of 2% from 2012 through 2016, compared with 6% for the rest of the industry, according to consultancy A.T. Kearney.[1]

The food and beverage industry is also embattled by changing tastes as more consumers look for fresh foods, with less artificial additives and with more organic ingredients. Company CEOs are facing a very new and challenging world. An industry insider told the *Wall Street Journal*, "You've got a lot of CEOs that are at their wit's end trying to figure out growth." In fact, the *Wall Street Journal* recently reported that food and beverage company CEOs are being replaced at an unprecedented rate. Since early 2017, at least 16 major packaged-food and beverage chief executives have stepped down. The departures include Denise Morrison of followed by CEO changes at General Mills Inc.,

1. Annie Gasparro and Jacob Bunge, "Food Companies Churn Through CEOs, Desperate for Fresh Ideas," *Wall Street Journal*, May 29, 2018.

Mondelez International Inc., Kellogg Co., Nestlé USA, Hershey Co., J.M. Smucker Co. and Twinkie-maker Hostess.[2]

In the past, big food and beverage companies were identified by their major brands and products: Kraft and cheese, Oscar Mayer and hot dogs, Post and cereal, Pepsi and soda. Using big marketing budgets and familiar themes, these companies dominated grocery store shelf space. Consumers looked for their favorite. brands, and the companies could easily pass along price increases to bolster profits when sales declined. During economic downturns, cheaper private label products would take a portion of market share, but when economic recoveries followed, consumers returned to their favorite brands.

Now, shifts toward simpler ingredients and shopping for food online, combined with a rise in niche, small brands and grocery-store brands, have destroyed this old playbook. Adding to this nightmare for industry participants is recent increases in costs.

J.M. Smucker Co. makes jellies and jams and is the maker of Folgers coffee and Jif peanut butter. Like all its competitors, Smucker's has experienced sales declines for many of its established brands, and its profitability it being hurt by higher costs. It has been faced with higher costs for producing and transporting their products as prices for certain ingredients rise along with freight expenses. This has required Smucker's to raise retail prices on some foods, just as consumers are already departing for alternative products with simpler and fresher ingredients.

The solution for Smucker's involves trying to revive its traditional food business, and expanding into nontraditional areas such as pet foods. In April 2018, Smucker's said it would buy Ainsworth Pet Nutrition LLC in a $1.7 billion acquisition—furthering its push into pet food—and that it would look to sell its baking business, which includes Pillsbury cake mixes and Hungry Jack pancake mix.[3]

Looking for new products is not limited to Smucker's. In fact, most food and beverage companies are looking for new products that address consumers' changing tastes.

Beverage companies, like food companies are also struggling to find the next big thing because their current offerings are stagnant. Like food companies, beverage makers are trying to address new consumer

2. Ibid.

demands by offering a drink that does more than quench a thirst. Money is pouring into developing beverages that claim to do much more than quench thirst. Companies are focusing on "enhanced" drinks that promise everything from better sleep to a more youthful complexion. While sales of such drinks are rising—up 11% in the past year to $3 billion, according to market-research firm Spins—hundreds of new ones are launched each year, and the majority fail within a couple of years. Finding success involves the right mix of funding, taste, health claims, and luck. Finding the next trend that will endure is very difficult.[4]

It can take several years to develop a recipe, find suppliers, and produce a new drink in large volumes. The new product also needs a brand and marketing campaign that delivers a compelling story that will drive demand. And the new concept must be proven before retailers are willing to give up precious shelf space to the new product. Even then, consumers' tastes can change quickly. Take, for example, sales of beverages containing aloe vera and turmeric, claimed to ward off indigestion and inflammation. After several years of explosive growth, sales are declining. For beverage companies the search for the next big winner continues.

In response to this new world, struggling food and beverage companies often use consulting companies to identify the next big trend and then to find new niche companies that can be acquired. Licensing is also playing a big role for food and beverage companies trying to change course and respond to their current challenges.

This new section reports the royalty rates associated with licensing in the food and beverage industry. The royalty rates reported in this new section are graphed below based on the number of times a royalty rate appeared in license deals. Some licenses involved more than one rate, depending on annual sales volume. Only rates specified as a percentage of sales have been included. Lump-sum payments, per unit rates, and one instance where the royalty base was gross profits are excluded from this chart.

The most common royalty rate is 2% of net sales. It is worth noting that over 80% of the negotiated royalty rates are 7% of sales or less, and 73% of the rates are 5% or less. The minority of royalty rates

3. Annie Gasparro and Allison Prang, "Smucker Forced to Raise Some Retail Prices to Counter Higher Costs Company Sees More Growth Potential in Pet Food, Now Its Largest Division," *Wall Street Journal*, November 7, 2018.

4. Annie Gasparro, "Many New Wonder Drinks Are All Wet," *Wall Street Journal*, August 29, 2018, B1.

that are above 7% must be assumed to be associated with products that yield an extraordinary profit margin atypical of the food and beverage industry profit margins.

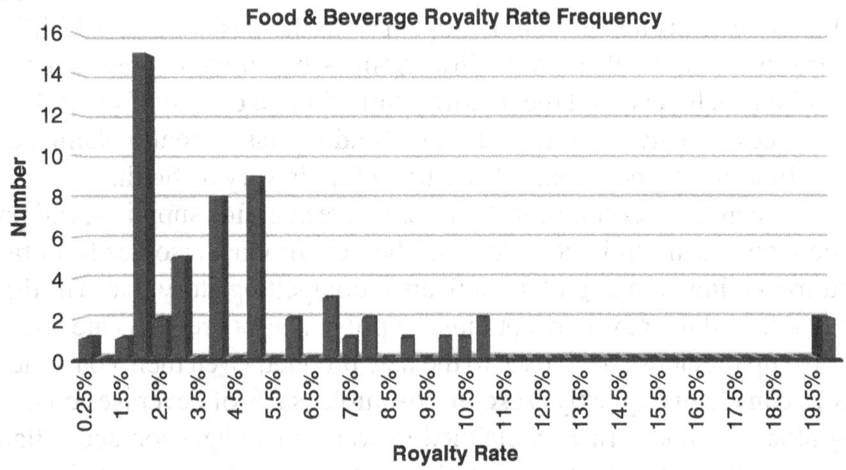

Details of the royalty rates appearing in the above chart follow.

MARIO ANDRETTI—5% ON SALES

Mario Andretti and AWG, Ltd. entered into a non-transferable, non-sub-licensable, worldwide license agreement in December of 1997, to use the "Andretti" name. In exchange, AWG will pay Andretti a royalty equal to 5% of the gross revenue from sales of wine products bearing his name, in addition to an annual payment equal to the lesser of either 2% of AWG profits or $150,000, on all wine label sales. The term of the agreement is perpetual.

Mario Andretti is one of the most decorated racecar drivers of all time. Born in Italy in 1940, he moved to the United States and began his racing career in 1959. He was an incredibly versatile driver, winning open car, drag racing, and stock car events. In 2000 he was awarded "Driver of the Century" by *Racer* magazine. In his illustrious career, he won the Indy 500, the Daytona 500, and driver of the year in three different decades.

AWG, Ltd. is a company formed for the production and marketing of wine, initially under the name of Mario Andretti.

BOTTLE DESIGN—"TRINITY"—8% OF SALES

Castle Brands, Inc. is an emerging developer and global marketer of premium branded spirits within four growing categories of the spirits industry: vodka, rum, Irish whiskey, and liqueurs/cordials. The company's premium spirits brands include brands that CBI owns, such as Boru vodka, Knappogue Castle Whiskey, the Clontarf Irish whiskeys, Sea Wynde rum, and Brady's Irish cream liqueur, brands for which the company possesses certain marketing and distribution rights, either directly or indirectly, including Goslings' rums, and Celtic Crossing liqueur and Pallini liqueurs, a brand that CBI distributes through an agency relationship.

Castle's unique "Trinity" bottle is the subject of Irish and UK utility patents owned by The Roaring Water Bay (Research & Development) Company Limited and a U.S. Design patent owned by CBI subsidiary, Castle Brands Spirits Company Limited. In December 2003, CBI entered into a license agreement with Roaring Water Bay (Research & Development) Company Limited whereby CBI obtained an exclusive license to use the patents for a five-year term ending in December 2008. The license agreement provides for a royalty equal to 8% of the net invoice price of Trinity bottle products covered by these patents sold or otherwise disposed of by the company, subject to a maximum of €30,000 per year. The license agreement also includes CBI's right to acquire the patent registrations for the Trinity bottle for €90,000.

Source: Castle Brands, Inc., 2006, 10K.

BIG LEAGUE CHEW—2.5% TO 5% OF SALES

Big League Chew is a shredded bubble gum product that lets kids make believe they are using chewing tobacco, just like their professional baseball heroes. The gum is shredded and comes in a foil pouch. The product was developed by Yankee ex-pitcher Jim Bouton, partly because he disliked the taste of chewing tobacco. Amurol, a subsidiary of Wrigley Company, pays royalties to manufacture and distribute the product ranging from 2.5% to 5% on sales.

BRITNEY SPEARS—9% OF SALES

Britney Brands, Inc. and Famous Fixins, Inc. signed an exclusive worldwide license agreement in October 1999 allowing FFI to use the "Britney

Spears" trade name in connection with bubble gum sold in a CD case. In return for the use of the Britney Spears trade name, FFI agreed to pay a royalty of 9% of net sales. In addition to the 9% royalty, FFI agreed to advance $150,000 payable as follows: $50,000 upon execution of the agreement, $25,000 by the end of the first year, and $75,000 due before the end of the agreement, all for the purpose of covering the minimum guaranteed amount. The term of the agreement is three years unless otherwise terminated.

Britney Brands, Inc. is a company that manages the trademark name of Britney Spears. Famous Fixins, Inc. is a manufacturer and distributor of celebrity food items and producer of various other consumer products.

BERGHOFF BEER TRADEMARK—$1.2 MILLION

General Beer, a liquor, wine, and beer distributor in Madison, Wisconsin, purchased the beer trademark Berghoff in September 1994 for $1.2 million from The Joseph Huber Brewing Company of Monroe, Wisconsin. In 1994 the brewery made and sold approximately 100,000 gallons of the beer, representing sales of $8 million. The Berghoff brand accounted for approximately 28% of the sales—approximately $2.2 million. The ratio of trademark value to annual revenues equals 55% of revenues. The Joseph Huber Brewing Company is currently in Chapter 11 reorganization.

Source: *Licensing Economics Review*, May 1996.

BEVERAGES—$0.25 (CDN.) PER CASE

Clearly Canadian Beverage Corp. produces and markets Clearly Canadian®, a line of natural mineral waters, and flavored sparkling water beverages. The company announced it had exercised its right to terminate its royalty and distribution agreement with Camfrey Resources Ltd. The company's termination of the agreement was effective December 31, 1992. In connection with the termination of the agreement, the company is required to pay a "royalty termination allowance" equal to five times the average annual royalty paid during the last two years of the current term of the agreement. Based on this royalty buy-out formula, the company has now paid $22,900,478 (Cdn.) to Camfrey. As a result of the termination, the company is no longer required to pay any royalties to Camfrey under the agreement. Previously, the company was required to pay a royalty of $0.25 (Cdn.) per case on sales of Clearly Canadian® products in the United States. The company's profitability has been enhanced by $0.25 (Cdn.) per case as a result of terminating the Camfrey royalty. The company has funded the payment of the royalty termination allowance through the liquidation of short-term investments, which were held for this purpose. Through distribution agreements, Clearly Canadian is sold throughout the United States, Canada, Japan, Great Britain, and Ireland.

Source: *Licensing Economics Review*, March 1993.

CHAMPIONLYTE—3% TO 6% ON SALES

Sara Lee Global Finance, LLC sued ChampionLyte Products, Inc. during 2001 claiming that the "ChampionLyte" trademark infringed upon the "Champion" sportswear trademark owned by Sara Lee. On April 1, 2003, a settlement was reached granting ChampionLyte an exclusive license to use the "ChampionLyte" trademark in connection with sugarfree drinks in the United States, Mexico, and Canada. The initial term of the licensing agreement is five years with the option to renew for two additional five-year terms. In exchange, for the right to use the trademark, ChampionLyte agrees to pay a 3% royalty until sales surpass $10,000,000 when it will become a 5% royalty payment, and finally when sales reach $15,000,000 it will become 6% royalty payment.

Contract Year	Minimum Royalty Payment
2003	$500,000
2004	$750,000
2005	$1,000,000
2006	$1,250,000
2007	$1,500,000
2008a	$2,000,000
2009	$2,500,000
2010	$3,000,000

(Continued)

2011	$3,500,000
2012	$4,000,000
2013b	$5,000,000
2014	$6,000,000
2015	$7,000,000
2016	$8,000,000
2017	$9,000,000

a. Contract will be renewed for a second five-year term if sales in 2005–2007 average at least $1,500,000.
b. Contract will be renewed for a third time if sales in 2010–2012 average at least $5,000,000.

Sara Lee Global Finance, LLC is a subsidiary of the Sara Lee Corporation. Sara Lee is a global manufacturer and marketer of consumer products with operations in 55 countries and markets in approximately 200 nations. Products manufactured and marketed by Sara Lee include baked goods, processed meat, beverage systems, coffee and tea, and various kinds of active wear, intimate clothing, and other apparel, and personal products, household products, and shoe products.

ChampionLyte Products, Inc. is a public company based in Florida. ChampionLyte is the first to release a completely sugar-free sports drink. ChampionLyte's subsidiary Old Fashioned Syrup Company manufactures, markets, and distributes three flavors of sugar-free syrups.

CHEESE—5% ON SALES

Galaxy Nutritional Foods, Inc. is principally engaged in developing, manufacturing, and marketing a variety of healthy cheese and dairy-related products, as well as other cheese alternatives, and is a leading producer of dairy alternative products made with soy. These healthy cheese and dairy-related products include low or no fat, no saturated fat, no trans-fat, low or no cholesterol, and lactose-free varieties. These products are sold throughout the United States and internationally to customers in the retail and food service markets.

GNF is the market leader within its alternative cheese category niche, but in being so, the category increases or decreases partly as a result of its marketing efforts. GNF believes that the greatest source of future growth in the cheese alternative category will come through customers shifting to cheese alternatives from natural cheese. Rather than focusing primarily on consumers with a preference or medical condition predisposing them to non-dairy cheese and comparing GNF products to other cheese alternative brands, the company intends to focus on educating cheese consumers on the healthy attributes of cheese alternatives versus traditional cheese.

Pursuant to an oral-contract manufacturing and distribution arrangement among GNF, Del Sunshine LLC, a Delaware limited liability company, and Non-Dairy Specialty Foods, LLC, a Nevada limited liability company and affiliate of Del, GNF began manufacturing certain private label products for Del and delivering them directly to Del's customers, including Del's major customer, WalMart, Inc. in April 2004. These private label products were produced using label and packaging trademarks owned by Del. Sales to Del accounted for 12% of GNF sales during fiscal 2005, which attributed to 65% of the increase in sales over fiscal 2004. The business with Del resulted in an account receivable owed to GNF of approximately $1,550,000 as of April 11, 2005. In the fourth quarter of fiscal 2005, GNF reserved nearly $1,550,000 in accounts receivable and wrote off $210,000 in inventory related to Del based upon the determination in April 2005 that collection from Del was questionable as of March 31, 2005.

On April 11, 2005, GNF executed with Del a Trademark License Agreement and an Assignment of Accounts Receivable Agreement. Pursuant to the Trademark License Agreement, Del licensed to GNF the rights in certain Del trademarks, which allowed GNF to sell products directly to Del's customers, including WalMart, Inc. and other food retailers, using such trademarks. In consideration for the license, GNF agreed to pay to Del a 5% royalty on the net sales of such products. In accordance with the Trademark License Agreement, GNF can offset any royalties that are owed to Del under the agreement against GNF's accounts receivable and other amounts owed to us by Del.

Source: Galaxy Nutritional Foods, Inc., 2005, 10K/A.

COOL LUC—4% OF SALES

In an exclusive license agreement dated November 1, 2002, Cool Luc LLC, through its wholly-owned subsidiary, entered into an agreement granting America Water Star, Inc. an exclusive license to make, use, and sell the Cool Luc brand for all markets and industries except for the Chicago Metropolitan Area and Michigan to us in an extreme energy drink marketed primarily in the Midwestern United States. American Water agreed to pay a royalty 4% of the gross revenues received for the licensed products sold.

Source: American Water Star, 2003, 10-K.

COMIC BOOK MILK—2.5% TO 11% OF SALES

Bravo Foods International Corp. is involved in the development and marketing of its own Slammers® trademarked brand, the obtaining of license rights from third-party holders of intellectual property rights to other trademarked brands, logos, and characters, and the granting of production and marketing rights to processor dairies to produce branded flavored milk utilizing its intellectual property. In the United States, Bravo generates revenue from the unit sales of branded flavored milks to retail consumer outlets. Currently, Bravo uses a single third-party processor in the United States to produce all of its single-serve milk-based beverages. Bravo recognizes revenue in the United States at the gross amount of invoices for the sale of finished product to wholesale buyers. Bravo takes title to its branded flavored milks when they are shipped by third-party processors and recognizes as revenue the gross wholesale price charged to wholesale customers.

Internationally, Bravo generates revenue primarily through the sale of "kits" to these processors. "Kits" sold to processors consist of flavor ingredients that are developed and refined by Bravo and the grant of production rights to processors to produce the flavored milks. The consideration paid to Bravo under these production contracts consists of fees charged for Bravo's grant of production rights for the branded flavored milks plus a charge for flavor ingredients. The fees charged by Bravo for the production rights are set to match royalty fees for its intellectual property licenses.

On February 4, 2005, Bravo entered into a two-year license agreement for the utilization of Marvel Heroes characters on Bravo's flavored milks in the United Kingdom and Ireland. Bravo agreed to a royalty rate of 4% of net wholesale sales in the territory against the prepayment of a guaranteed minimum royalty amount. Bravo has adopted the unit sales model currently used in the United States. Bravo has outsourced the infrastructure required for the production, promotion, marketing, distribution, and sale of its products through a production agreement with Waterfront Corporation in the UK and through an exclusive sales agency agreement with Drinks Brokers, Ltd. a UK registered company responsible for the launch and growth of several major beverage brands in the licensed territory.

In March 2005, Bravo entered into a new one-year license agreement with Marvel Enterprises, Inc. to use its Super Hero® properties to promote Bravo's branded milk products in the United States, Canada and Mexico. Under the terms of the license agreement, Bravo agreed to a royalty rate of 5% of net wholesale sales in the United States, 4% for school lunch channels, and 2.5% for school hot lunch programs. Bravo also agreed to a 11% royalty on the amount invoiced to dairy processors for "kits" in Canada and Mexico.

On February 4, 2005, Bravo entered into an 18-month license agreement for the utilization of Marvel Heroes characters on its flavored milks in nine Middle East Countries. Bravo agreed to a 11% royalty on the amount invoiced to third-party dairy processors for "kits" in the territory against the prepayment of a guaranteed minimum royalty amount.

Source: Bravo Foods International, Corp., 2005, 10-KSB.

CRICKET WORLD CUP SPONSORSHIP—$3.69 MILLION

Coca-Cola Co. has accused rival U.S. soft drink maker PepsiCo Inc. of infringing on its sponsorship rights to the Cricket World Cup. Coca-Cola said it spent $3.69 million to become the official soft drink supplier for the month-long tournament.

Source: *Licensing Economics Review*, January 1996.

DETHRONE ENERGY DRINK—5% TO 12% OF GROSS PROFITS

On March, 2012, Dethrone Royalty Inc. granted a worldwide exclusive license to a related party, To Sports Innovation, Inc. for use of the

"Dethrone Royalty and Dethrone" marks for use in the manufacture and sales of sports performance or energy drinks.

Dethrone Royalty Inc. has given the licensee the right to use the Dethrone trademark worldwide in connection with the manufacture and sale of sports performance or energy drinks along with any other non-alcoholic beverage under the trade name, Dethrone Beverages.

The license agreement is for five years.

The license requires payments from To Sports as follows for the five years of the agreement:

1. 12% of Gross Profit
2. $50,000 plus 8% of Gross Profit
3. $100,000 or 6% of Gross profit, whichever is higher
4. $150,000 or 6% of Gross profit, whichever is higher
5. $200,000 or 6% of Gross profit, whichever is higher

Source: Exclusive Building Services, Inc., 2012, 8-K.

DAIRY BRAND—2% OF SALES

Dutch Lady Milk Industries Berhad entered into a licensing agreement in December 2001 with Friesland Brands BV of the Netherlands for the use of proprietary intellectual property, including trademarks and technology, and the provision of technical assistance. Under the five-year agreement, Dutch Lady Milk Industries will pay Friesland Brands BV a running royalty of 2% of net sales after deductions for Malaysian taxes.

Friesland Coberco Dairy Foods started as a farmers' cooperative with roots going back to 1894. After many mergers and takeovers, Friesland Coberco Dairy Foods has become a multinational company with 6,700 employees operating from 94 branches worldwide. Friesland Coberco Dairy Foods develops, produces, and sells a wide range of branded dairy products and fruits-based drinks for the consumer market, professional users, and food producers. Their names include, but are not limited to: Appelsientje, CoolBest, Completa, and Dutch Lady/Bella Holandesa.

Dutch Lady Milk Industries Berhad—while in nearly all countries the company name is "Friesland," in Malaysia the Friesland subsidiary does business under the name Dutch Lady Milk Industries, formally known as Dutch Baby Milk Industries. The company's principal activities include the manufacturing of sweetened condensed milk, milk powder, dairy products, and fruit juice drinks for distribution in the home market (Malaysia) and for export.

DAIRY PRODUCTS—2% ON NET SALES

Dutch Lady Milk Industries Berhad was granted a five-year license from Friesland Brands B.V. to use proprietary intellectual property, including trademarks and know-how. Friesland Brands will also provide Dutch Lady Milk with technical assistance. Dutch Lady Milk will be the sole Malaysian licensee of Friesland's branding. Under the agreement, Friesland will receive a royalty equivalent to 2% of net sales after withholdings for Malaysian taxes.

Friesland Brands B.V. is a wholly owned subsidiary of the Dutch company, Friesland Coberco Dairy Foods, which develops, produces and sells a variety of branded dairy products and fruit-based drinks. The company was formed in its current state in 1997 with the merger of four large dairy cooperatives: Coberco, Friesland Dairy Foods, Twee Provicien, and De Zuid-Oost-Hoek. The company has a strong presence in Western Europe, Central Europe, Western Africa, and Southeast Asia. Friesland Coperco operating companies carry out operations in these areas.

Dutch Lady Milk Industries Berhad is a Malaysian company that produces and sells sweetened condensed milk, milk powder, dairy products, and fruit juice drinks. The company, Dutch Baby Milk, was established in 1965 to replace imported sweetened condensed milk with domestically produced products. Since its establishment, the company has expanded its product line to include full cream milk, yogurts, and sterilized milk. In 1983, the company changed its name from Dutch Baby Milk to Dutch Lady.

Source: *Licensing Economics Review*, December 2001.

DANNON/YOCREAM CO-BRAND—4% ON SALES

Dannon Company, Inc. and Yocream International, Inc. entered into a license agreement on September 6, 2001. giving Yocream a non-transferable, non-assignable license to use the co-brand name "Dannon/YoCream" for the marketing, manufacture, and sale of soft frozen yogurt in the United States. In exchange for the co-brand, Yocream agrees to pay Dannon 4% of net sales of the soft frozen yogurt sold under the co-brand. The term of the license will be for five years with the option to renew if mutual agreement is reached one year prior to the expiration of the agreement.

Dannon Company, Inc. is a subsidiary of the Danone Group. Danone is a worldwide leader in water and fresh dairy products. As of December 31, 2002, Danone had approximately $16.88 billion in sales and employed a worldwide workforce of approximately 95,000 employees.

Yocream International, Inc. makes, markets, and sells frozen yogurt, sorbet, frozen custard, smoothie, and ice cream products in a variety of non-fat, low fat, and premium flavors. These products are distributed to yogurt shops, fast food chains, discount club warehouses, convenience stores, restaurants, hospitals, school districts, food distributors, military installations, and other types of businesses and outlets. The company's primary brand is "Yocream," and it has many products that fall under the "Yocream" trademark.

DAVE MIRRA—7% ON SALES

Famous Fixins, Inc. (FFI) is a manufacturer and distributor of celebrity food items and producer of various other consumer products. On December 22, 1999, Dave Mirra, a professional BMX biker, and FFI signed a worldwide license agreement allowing FFI to use "Dave Mirra" as a trade name for a line of chewing gum and cereal. In return, FFI agreed to pay Dave Mirra 7% of the gross receipts less trade and quantity discounts. In addition, Dave Mirra received a warrant to purchase 25,000 shares of FFI unregistered common stock at the exercise price of $.20 per share. The term of the agreement is three years, and FFI has the right of first refusal regarding renewal of the license.

Dave Mirra has won 14 medals in his career, 11 of which are gold medals from the X-Games.

DEL SUNSHINE—5% OF NET SALES

Galaxy Nutritional Foods, Inc. develops and globally markets plant-based cheese and dairy alternatives, as well as processed organic cheese and cheese food to grocery and natural foods retailers, mass merchandisers, and food service accounts. The company's overall strategy is to enhance the value of the Galaxy Nutritional Foods' brands by developing nutritious products that meet the taste and dietary needs of today's increasingly health-conscious consumers.

Veggie, the leading brand in the cheese alternative category of the grocery channel and Galaxy's top selling product group, is primarily merchandised in the produce section and provides calcium and protein without cholesterol, saturated fat, or trans fat. In the natural foods channel, our brands include Rice, Veggy, Vegan, and Wholesome Valley, which are primarily merchandised in the cheese alternative or dairy sections. The company also has Galaxy imitation and private label products, including processed slices and shreds. These products are primarily sold in the grocery, mass markets, and food service channels.

Galaxy sells its products through leading grocery store chains including Publix, Kroger, Safeway, Albertson's, Wakefern, H.E. Butt, and natural food stores including Whole Foods, Wild Oats, and several independents. Galaxy seeks to build core brand recognition and a broader consumer base through marketing, including product sampling and advertising programs to educate consumers on the benefits of healthier eating.

Pursuant to an oral contract manufacturing and distribution arrangement among Galaxy, Del Sunshine LLC, a Delaware limited liability company, and Non-Dairy Specialty Foods, LLC, a Nevada limited liability company and affiliate of Del, Galaxy began manufacturing certain private label products for Del and delivering them directly to Del's customers, including Del's major customer, Wal-Mart, Inc. in April 2004. These private label products were produced using label and packaging trademarks owned by Del. Sales to Del accounted for 12% of our sales during fiscal 2005, which attributed to 65% of the increase in sales over fiscal 2004.

On April 11, 2005, Galaxy executed with Del a trademark license agreement and an Assignment of Accounts Receivable Agreement. Pursuant to the trademark license agreement, Del licensed to Galaxy the rights in certain Del trademarks, which allowed Galaxy to sell products directly to Del's customers, including Wal-Mart, Inc. and other food retailers, using such trademarks. In consideration for the license, Galaxy agreed to pay to Del a 5% royalty on the net sales of such products.

Source: Galaxy Nutritional Foods, Inc., 2006, 10K.

DISNEY CHARACTERS WATER—4% OF NET SALES

On March 31,2012, True Drinks Holdings, Inc. entered into a license agreement with Disney Consumer Products, Inc. in order to obtain rights for a three-year term to feature popular Disney characters on AquaBall™ Naturally Flavored Water, allowing AquaBall™ to stand out among other beverages marketed towards children.

Under the terms and conditions of the licensing agreements, the parties to the license will create colorful, eye-catching labels that surround the entire spherical shape of each AquaBall™. Once the label designs are approved, True Drinks works with Disney to set retail calendars, rotating the placement of different AquaBall™ designs over the course of the year.

The terms of the Disney licensing agreement stipulate a royalty rate of 4% on the sales of AquaBall Naturally Flavored Water adorned with Disney characters, paid quarterly, with a total royalty guarantee of $231,600 over the term of the agreement, which has a term ending date of March 31, 2015. In addition, True Holdings is required to spend 1% of sales on advertising and promotional opportunities and is required to make common marketing fund contributions totaling $96,188 over the life of the agreement.

Source: True Drinks Holdings, Inc., 2013, 10-K.

EGGS—$0.01 PER POUND TO $0.05 PER DOZEN

A new line of eggs with increased polyunsaturated fats was licensed at a royalty of $0.05 per carton of a dozen eggs. Sales of egg byproducts require a royalty of $0.01 per pound. Vitafort International Corporation is a company that designs nutritionally enhanced food and beverage products and then develops integrated processing and marketing procedures. Vitafort granted the license to Nulaid Food Inc., which is an egg producer on the West Coast. The eggs will be sold under the Vitafort name.

Source: *Licensing Economics Review*, September 1990.

F.I.T.T. ENERGY BEVERAGE – $0.05 PER BOTTLE

F.I.T.T. Energy Products, Inc. is in the business of the manufacturing (on an outsource basis), distribution, and sale of energy shots. F.I.T.T. was formed in January 2010, and its current product line consists of three 2-ounce energy shots. Two of the energy shots ("F.I.T.T. Energy Extreme" and "F.I.T.T. Energy Rx") were funded and developed by the company. While the company funded the third energy shot, named "F.I.T.T. Energy for Life" ("FITT Original"), it was developed by FITT Highway Products, Inc. ("FHWY"), a separate public company traded on the OTCQB under the trading symbol FHWY.

On August 12, 2010, the company entered into an operating agreement with FHWY under which F.I.T.T. is performing the majority of their operating functions using capital raised by F.I.T.T. FHWY, which has significant debt and no cash, was unable to enter into agreements with third parties to perform basic operating functions such as marketing, production, and distribution due to a number of factors including its poor financial condition. Under the operating agreement F.I.T.T. is obligated to pay FHWY a royalty of $0.05 per bottle sold of "F.I.T.T. Energy for Life." F.I.T.T.'s CEO is also the CEO of FHWY and certain of its shareholders are also shareholders of FHWY.

Source: F.I.T.T. Energy Products, Inc., 2014, 8K.

FOOD FLAVOR—$30 MILLION DEVELOPMENT COST PLUS 1% TO 4% OF SALES

Several big food and beverage companies are looking at a new ingredient in the battle for health-conscious consumers: a chemical that tricks the taste buds into sensing sugar or salt even when it is not there.

Kraft Foods, Nestlé, Coca-Cola, and Campbell Soup are all working with a biotechnology company called Senomyx, Inc., which has developed several chemicals, most of which do not have any flavor of their own but instead work by activating or blocking receptors in the mouth that are responsible for taste. They can enhance or replicate the taste of sugar, salt, and monosodium glutamate (MSG) in foods. By adding one of Senomyx's flavorings to their products, manufacturers can, for instance, reduce the sugar in a cookie or salt in a can of soup by one-third to one-half while retaining the same sweetness or saltiness.

Kraft, Nestlé, Coca-Cola, and Campbell Soup have contracted with Senomyx for exclusive rights to use the ingredients in certain types of food and beverages, although the companies declined to identify those categories. Since Senomyx's flavor compounds will be used in small proportions (less than one part per million), the company is able to bypass the lengthy FDA approval process required to get food additives on the market. Getting the Flavor and Extract Manufacturers Association status of generally recognized as safe (GRAS) certification took Senomyx less than 18 months, including a three-month safety study using rats. In contrast, the maker of the artificial sweetener sucralose spent 11 years winning FDA approval and is required to list the ingredient on food labels.

According to filings with the Securities and Exchange Commission, Kraft Foods, Nestlé, Coca-Cola, and Campbell Soup have collectively paid Senomyx $30 million to finance research and development. When the flavorings are incorporated into foods, Senomyx has said it will collect royalties of 1% to 4% of a product's sales.

Source: Melanie Warner, "Food Companies Test Flavorings That Can Mimic Sugar, Salt and MSG," *New York Times*, April 6, 2005.

FOOD FLAVOR—$20 MILLION DEVELOPMENT COST PLUS 1% TO 4% OF SALES

In August 2009, Senomyx, Inc. entered into a Collaborative Research, Development, Commercialization and License Agreement with the Swiss licensee, Firmenich SA, for novel flavor ingredients intended to provide a sweet enhancement taste effect of sucrose, fructose, or various forms of rebaudioside in select product categories on a worldwide basis. The agreement provides Firmenich with exclusive rights on the development and commercialization of existing and newly discovered flavor ingredients for all forms of foods and beverages for human consumption, excluding gum, sugar confections, and chocolate confections and non-alcoholic beverages. The agreement also provides Firmenich with co-exclusive rights with respect to non-alcoholic dry powdered beverages.

Senomyx received an initial license fee payment of $10 million from Firmenich following execution of the agreement in August 2009. Firmenich also agreed to fund a portion of Senomyx's ongoing research under the agreement for a minimum of two years, with three consecutive options of one year each that could further extend the collaborative research funding period at consecutively higher funding rates. In addition, Firmenich agreed to pay Senomyx a second $10 million license fee within 30 days following regulatory approval of the first flavor ingredient that Firmenich selects for development and determines to be commercially viable.

The agreement also calls for Senomyx to receive royalties of up to 4% on its collaborator's sales of retail and food service products, and in some cases higher on the collaborator's sales of ingredient supplies containing flavor ingredients. The actual royalties payable vary by agreement and depend on a number of factors including, for example, the product field, cost of goods savings, degree of flavor enhancement, and sales volume of collaborator products incorporating a flavor ingredients.

Source: Senomyx, Inc., 2009, 10-Q.

FRENCH FRIES/VENDING—5% OF SALES

Tasty Fries, Inc. developed a patented French fries vending machine. The company intends to manufacture and market the machine in both domestic and international markets through a combination of exclusive territorial distributorships and traditional sales to established companies in the vending industry. The company may also own and operate machines itself. The machines are expected to be located in high-traffic locations that have historically been successful for vending operators, such as universities, airports, bus and train stations, high schools, military bases, industrial locations and recreational venues.

The company has also developed a related proprietary potato product for the production of French fries in the machine. Although the company has developed its own potato product, the company presently intends to purchase a comparable potato product, for use in the machine, from a third party. This strategic determination is driven by the high costs associated with establishing a production line to produce its own proprietary potato product.

The company's basic business strategy is to market the machines and the ancillary products that are required to prepare each serving of French fries. These ancillary products include the potato product, vegetable cooking oil, serving cups, and condiments. The company's long-term profitability and success will be driven primarily by the revenue and accompanying profit to the company associated with each and every vended portion sold from its installed base of machines.

Tasty Fries, Inc., formerly Adelaide Holdings, Inc. announced that an award in the American Arbitration Association matter *California*

Food and Vending v. Tasty Fries, Inc. et al. has been rendered against Tasty Fries in the aggregate amount of $279,500 for domestic and international distribution fees owed to California Food and Vending. An additional $249,500 in compensatory damages has also been awarded. The arbitration award also ordered (a) the enforcement of the terms of previously negotiated agreements which, generally, provide for the payment by the company of certain royalties, fees, and profits to CFV in connection with the future sale of Tasty Fries vending machines and related products; and (b) the issuance by Tasty Fries to CFV of an option for the purchase of 2,000,000 shares of Tasty 'Fries' common stock at an exercise price of $2.00 per share through March 17, 1997.

Source: *Licensing Economics Review*, October 1994.

June 1999 Update Litigation between Tasty Fries, Inc. and California Food & Vending, Inc. was concluded with what company officials termed "a complete resolution of all issues between the two companies in a manner wholly beneficial to Tasty Fries." California Food & Vending had contended in a lawsuit filed in Federal District Court in California that Tasty Fries had not complied with the parties' prior settlement agreement. Tasty Fries counter-sued California Food & Vending, charging that it had breached its fiduciary responsibility as Tasty Fries' distributor by failing to market and promote the French fry vending machine and by unsuccessfully attempting to introduce its own machine. In resolving the case, Tasty Fries regained its State of California distributorship, which was owned by California Food & Vending.

California is regarded by industry sources as the most potentially lucrative territory in the United States for French fry vending machines, with 17% of the anticipated domestic market. In addition, California Food & Vending completely gave up its rights to share equally in the first $4,000,000 of international and domestic distributorship fees to be paid to Tasty Fries when it commences the commercial delivery of its machines and 25% of all such fees paid to Tasty Fries after the first $4,000,000. Tasty Fries also received a 10% reduction from $500 per machine to $450 per machine with respect to the royalty to be paid to CFV on the anticipated $9,000 cost of the machines.

The Tasty Fries™ vending machines are revolutionary in design. The multi-patented machines prepare, cook, and dispense French fries with the flavor, aroma, and texture of freshly cut French fries. Total vend time is less than 90 seconds. The fries are made from top quality Idaho russet potatoes, and are cooked in cholesterol-free oil using state-of-the-art robotics technology. The machines will be located worldwide in strategic high-traffic areas like airports, universities, bus and train stations, military bases, theaters, office buildings, and schools, and in work and recreational venues.

HAWAIIAN TROPIC—4% OF SALES

In an agreement dated January 1, 2003, American Star Water, Inc. was granted rights to produce, market, and sell, on an exclusive basis in the United States and Canada, items bearing the Hawaiian Tropic trademark for a period of three years for licensed goods of flavored bottled water only.

Hawaiian Tropic is a trademark used to identify sun-tanning oils and lotions, sun and wind screens, skin moisturizers and moisteners for tan preservation, sunburn ointments, shampoos, hair conditioners, hand and body lotions, lip balms, T-shirts, swimwear, and sportswear. The licensor produces sun care products. It offers tanning products, such as tanning oils, tanning lotions, and indoor tanning products.

The beverages bearing the trademark are sugar free, no carb, caffeine free, sodium free tropical drinks. Flavors include Strawberry Kiwi, Lemon Lime, Orange Guava and Pineapple Grapefruit in United States and Canada.

As consideration for the license, American Water Star will pay Tanning Research Laboratories, Inc. a royalty of 4% of invoice sales (net of shipping and sales taxes), payable each quarter.

Source: American Water Star, Inc., 2003, 10-K.

HEALTHY FOOD—CASH, STOCK, AND 10% OF SALES

American Consolidated Management Group, Inc. (ACMG) is involved in the development and commercialization of natural plant products for use by established food manufacturers in their products aimed at the fast-growing Functional Foods segment of the estimated $900 billion United States domestic food industry. ACMG's first priority and primary goal is in the commercialization of a natural, organic, fruit and vegetable powder that is designed to be added to any food processing application so that the food product utilizing this powder can make the claim that one serving would contain the equivalent nutrient value of three to five servings of fruits and vegetables.

The current Food Guide Pyramid put out by the United States Department of Agriculture (USDA) recommends, for a healthy diet, the consumption of five servings of vegetables and four servings of fruit every day. Current recommendations from the American Institute for Cancer Research and the American Heart Association are more than double these amounts. The problem is that the consumption of fruits and vegetables in the United States and much of the developed world is decreasing. As a result of the work done by Dr. Jack Watkins over the past 10 years, ACMG believes that Dr. Watkins has developed a method so that the phytonutrients contained in fruits and vegetables can be naturally stabilized for inclusion in almost any processed food product and at the same time extend the shelf life of these phytonutrients.

On March 23, 2004, the company entered into a license agreement with Beta Foods, LLC. The company has obtained an exclusive license to enhance, commercialize, manufacture, and market the all-natural plant product compound (the trade secret technology) developed by Dr. Jack Watkins in the United States, Mexico, Central America, Canada, and all countries in the European Union for a term of 50 years. In consideration for the license, the company agreed to pay Beta Foods, LLC (i) a 10% royalty on product sales, (ii) $300,000, and (iii) 2,500,000 shares of the Company's restricted stock, which payment has not been paid and which shares have not yet been issued. Approximately 25% of Beta Foods, LLC is beneficially owned by family members of Mr. George Mappin, a director and officer of the company; approximately 25% of Beta Foods, LLC is beneficially owned by Mr. Herschel Walker, a director and officer of the Company; and approximately 25% of Beta Foods, LLC is beneficially owned by family members of Mr. Richard Shanks, a shareholder of the company.

Source: American Consolidated Management Group, Inc., 2005, 10KSB.

ICE DRAFT—$5 MILLION

Anheuser-Busch was awarded $5 million by a federal jury in a trademark dispute with Canada's Labatt Breweries over ice-brewed beer. Labatt had claimed that it invented ice beer and that Anheuser-Busch copied the idea. Ice beer is a competitive new beer category, and several brewers have rolled out their own versions. The Canadian firm sued Anheuser-Busch for $61 million, or triple the amount it says it lost as a result of the St. Louis–based brewer's introduction of an ice beer. Anheuser-Busch, maker of Budweiser, had sought $13.5 million in damages from Labatt. Labatt argued it had an exclusive right to terms such as "ice," "ice beer," and "ice brewed." And it claimed Anheuser-Busch only became interested in the concept after a meeting with Labatt executives in March 1993. Anheuser-Busch introduced Ice Draft from Budweiser in February 1994. It recently announced it was changing the name of the beer to Bud Ice. A light version will be called Bud Ice Light. Brewers such as Miller and Molson monitored the trial closely. Each is involved in a similar suit pending in federal court in Detroit.

Source: *Licensing Economics Review*, March 1995.

KRISPY KREME—2% ON SALES

HDN Development Corporation and Krispy Kreme Doughnuts, Inc. signed a non-exclusive, non-assignable, worldwide trademark license agreement in 1996 allowing Krispy Kreme to use all of the various trademarks and trade names associated with "Krispy Kreme" stores in connection with its manufacturing, packaging, selling, marketing, and distribution. In return for the use of trademarks and trade names, Krispy Kreme will pay 2% of all sales of licensed products and if Krispy Kreme is to sublicense any of the trademarks or names they would be payable to HDN as franchise fees. In addition, HDN will pay 25% of the franchise fees collected back to Krispy Kreme in consideration for the materials, marketing, knowhow, and effort expended by Krispy Kreme. The initial term of the agreement is one year and will automatically renew at the end of each year unless HDN or Krispy Kreme is found in breach.

HDN Development Corporation is the owner of the rights, title and interest to various trademarks including trademarks associated with Krispy Kreme doughnuts.

Krispy Kreme Doughnuts, Inc. is a specialty retailer of doughnuts baked daily on premises in Krispy Kreme stores. Krispy Kreme's principal business is the owning and franchising of Krispy Kreme retail stores. The typical store has the ability to produce 20 varieties of donuts and between 4,000 and 6,000 donuts daily. The doughnuts produced in the stores are then either sold in house or off premises.

MARVEL'S AVENGERS ASSEMBLE CHARACTERS—5% OF SALES

A licensing agreement, dated December 31, 2013, between True Drinks Holdings, Inc. and Marvel Characters B.V. allows True Drinks to feature popular characters on AquaBall™ Naturally Flavored Water to stand out among other beverages marketed towards children. AquaBall™ bottles will be sold featuring Marvel's Avengers Assemble characters, including Iron Man, Hulk, Captain America, and Thor.

Under the terms and conditions of the licensing agreement, True Drinks will work with the Marvel team to create colorful, eye-catching labels that surround the entire spherical shape of each AquaBall™ bottle.

The rights granted apply to the beverage industry and run for 18 months.

The terms of the agreement stipulates a royalty rate of 5% on the sales of AquaBall Naturally Flavored Water adorned with Marvel characters.

Source: Marvel Characters, 2013, 10-K.

MARVEL'S HEROES FLAVORED MILK—2% TO 4% OF SALES

On January 1, 2005, Bravo Foods International Corp. entered into a two-year non-exclusive license agreement for the utilization of Marvel Heroes characters on flavored milks in the United Kingdom and Ireland.

Marvel Heroes Classic Characters include Classic Marvel artwork for the co-mingled character program known as Marvel Heroes and taken only and exclusively from the dedicated Marvel Heroes Style Guide, as in effect from time to time during the term of the agreement, featuring the character families of Spider Man, X-Men, Hulk, Fantastic Four, Silver Surfer, Captain America, Thor, Iron Man, Daredevil, Namor, Dr. Strange, and Nick Fury, as well as other character as may be added to this program and featured in its style guide from time to time.

Marvel Heroes is specifically a co-mingled character program meaning that all Marvel Heroes licenses shall feature multiple characters in either of the two following ways: (a) not less than three equally represented characters on a single SKU, for example a bed duvet, T-shirt, or play-tent) or, subject to Marvel approval in writing on a case-by-case basis, (b) not less than four characters, one character per SKU, equally represented on a repeat purchase collectible SKU line (for example ball-point pens, lollipops) whereby the product line is conceived, branded, marketed, packaged, and merchandised as a collectible multiple character product line at all times.

The license applies to Extended Shelf Life and Aseptic UHT Flavored Milk— limited to the following sizes: 8 oz., 11.2 oz., and 16 oz.

Bravo has agreed to pay 2% of net sales of sales made directly to consumers and 4% of net sales in all other instances; 4% shall be added to royalty rate if licensed articles are sold F.O.B.

Source: Bravo Foods International Corp., 2005, 10-KSB.

MARVEL'S HEROES FLAVORED MILK IN THE MIDDLE EAST—11% OF SALES

On February 4, 2005, Bravo Foods International Corp. entered into an 18-month license agreement for the utilization of Marvel Heroes characters on flavored milks in the Middle East in conjunction with its execution of third-party production agreements for the manufacture and sale of its products in Saudi Arabia and Oman.

Bravo agreed to a 11% royalty on the amount invoiced to third-party dairy processors for kits in the territory against the prepayment of a guaranteed minimum royalty amount.

The agreement was not renewed for this License Agreement owing to the failure of our Marvel co-branded products to achieve expected market penetration.

Source: Bravo Foods International Corp., 2006, SB-2.

MEATBALLS—1% TO 6% OF NET SALES

On March 1, 2010, MamaMancini s Holdings Inc. was assigned a Development and License agreement. Under the terms of the agreement, the licensor shall develop for MamaMancini's a line of beef meatballs with sauce, turkey meatballs with sauce, and other similar meats and sauces for commercial manufacture, distribution, and sale. Licensor shall work with MamaMancini's to develop products that are acceptable to MamaMancini's. Upon acceptance of a product by MamaMancini's, the licensor's trade secret recipes, formulas, methods, and ingredients for the preparation and production of such products (the "Recipes") shall be subject to this Development and License Agreement.

The term of the agreement shall consist of the Exclusive Term and the Non-Exclusive Term. The Exclusive Term began on January 1, 2009, and ends on the 50th anniversary of the effective date, unless terminated or extended as provided herein. MamaMancini's may extend the Exclusive Term for an additional twenty-five (25) years, by notice in writing to Licensor, delivered on or before the 50th anniversary of the Effective Date. The Non-Exclusive Term begins upon expiration of the Exclusive Term and continues indefinitely thereafter.

During the Exclusive Term and the Non-Exclusive Term MamaMancini's will pay a royalty equal to the royalty rate, multiplied by MamaMancini's "Net Sales," where "Net Sales" means gross invoiced sales of products, directly or indirectly, to unrelated third parties, less (a) discounts (including cash discounts), and retroactive price reductions or allowances actually allowed or granted from the billed amount (collectively "Discounts"); (b) credits, rebates, and allowances actually granted upon claims, rejections, or returns, including recalls (voluntary or otherwise) (collectively, "Credits"); (c) freight, postage, shipping, and insurance charges; (d) taxes, duties, or other governmental charges levied on or measured by the billing amount, when included in billing, as adjusted for rebates and refunds; and (e) provisions for uncollectible accounts determined in accordance with reasonable accounting methods, consistently applied.

The Royalty Rate shall be: 6% of net sales up to $500,000 of net sales for each agreement year; 4% of net sales from $500,000 up to $2,500,000 of net sales for each agreement year; 2% of net sales from $2,500,000 up to $20,000,000 of net sales for each agreement year; and 1% of net sales in excess of $20,000,000 of net sales for each agreement year.

Source: Commitments and Contingencies, https://www.sec.gov/Archives/edgar/data/1520358/000149315217014609/R16.htm.

MEXICO WATER AND FRUIT DRINKS—2% OF SALES

On January 1, 2003, Panamerican Beverages SA DE CV, a Mexican licensor, granted to Panamco Golfo SA DE CV, a Mexican licensee, a related party, exclusive, transferable, sub-licensable right and license to fully use and exploit the trademarks throughout the territory of the licensed territory of the Republic of Mexico in connection with the manufacturing, marketing, and sale of purified water and fruit beverage.

The trademarks include trademarks in the International Class 32 under the registration numbers 436643 Risco, 455234 Risco and Design, 458791 Water Container Design, and certain other trademarks.

The parties have arranged and agreed to permit licensee to prepare, package, and sell within the licensed territory, a purified water and a fruit-flavored beverage under the trademarks.

The term of this agreement shall commence on the January 1, 2003, and shall expire on December 31, 2012. Licensed territory is the Golfo territory of the Republic of Mexico.

The licensee will pay to the licensor an annual royalty computed as 2% of the net selling price from the sale of purified water and fruit beverage sold under the Trademarks within the territory.

Source: Panamerican Beverages Inc, 2003, 10-Q.

MR. PEANUT SNACKS – $0.02 PER GALLON

Lincoln Snack Co. entered into a license agreement with Nabisco Ltd. for rights to use the Planters and Mr. Peanut trademark for use in Canada. Lincoln plans to use the acquired rights in connection with the manufacture, distribution, advertising, and sale of its Fiddle Faddle branded snack food products.

Nabisco granted the rights on a royalty-free basis for the first two years. In the third through fifth year Lincoln will pay (i) 1% of annual net sales and (ii) 2% of annual net sales of products in the distribution channels in the territory with respect to sales in excess of 500,000 equivalent cases of product.

Source: Lincoln Snacks Co., 1997, 10-Q.

NEW LEAF BRANDS BEVERAGE – 4% OF NET SALES

New Leaf Brands, Inc. is a diversified beverage holding company acquiring brands, distributors, and manufacturers within the beverage industry. New Leaf's strategy follows the initial success of the company's award-winning New Leaf Brands ready-to-drink teas and lemonades. The company intends to continue to market broadly its New Leaf branded products as well as acquire additional regional beverage brands in complementary categories. As part of New Leaf's brand acquisition strategy, it will acquire a portfolio of branded proprietary products, with distinctive packaging and deep regional appeal.

Using a two-step process, the company evaluates intangible assets for potential impairment on an annual basis or whenever events or circumstances indicate that impairment may have occurred. The first step of the impairment test, used to identify potential impairment, compares the estimated fair value of the intangible with the related carrying amount. If the estimated fair value of the intangibles exceeds its carrying amount, the intangible is not considered to be impaired, and the second step is unnecessary.

During the quarter that ended September 30, 2011, the company determined that a triggering event had occurred and performed an interim impairment analysis. The interim impairment analysis resulted in an impairment of $1,100,000 for the third quarter of 2011. During the year that ended December 31, 2011, the company determined that the economic uncertainty surrounding the company's ability to remain in business triggered an impairment analysis. The company's interim and annual tests predominately used a discounted cash flow model derived from internal budgets in assuming fair values for the impairment testing. Factors that could change the result of its impairment test include, but are not limited to, different assumptions used to forecast future net sales, expenses, capital expenditures and resources, and liquidity and working capital requirements used in New Leaf's cash flow models. In addition, selection of a risk-adjusted discount rate on the estimated undiscounted cash flow is susceptible to future changes in market conditions, and when these changes are unfavorable, they can adversely affect the original estimates of fair value.

The company's key assumptions used in its annual impairment analysis included the following: a discount rate of 18% based on the estimated weighted average cost of capital from the market participant point of view; a royalty rate of 4.0%; an average perpetual growth rate of 66% for six years; and a tax rate of 38%. An increase in the discount rate of 1% or a 1% deterioration of the perpetual revenue growth rate would increase the impairment loss by approximately \$38,000 or \$11,000, respectively. The company bases its fair value estimates on assumptions it believes to be reasonable, but which are unpredictable and inherently uncertain. For the year ended December 31, 2011, the impairment of the 'company's brand value mainly resulted in the decline in its projected revenues and operating results and cash flows. The company has concluded that impairment had existed at December 31, 2011, and has recorded an impairment charge, measured as the amount by which the carrying amount of the long-lived asset exceeds its fair value, of \$2,155,000 for the year ended December 31, 2011. In conjunction with preparing the revised forecasts, the company reevaluated the remaining estimated useful lives of the long-lived intangibles and concluded there is no change in its estimated remaining useful lives.

Source: New Leaf Brands Inc., 2012, 10Q.

PACKAGING/BEVERAGE CONTAINER – STOCK PLUS 2% OF GROSS PROFITS

Norpac Technologies, Inc. is in the business of developing and marketing a patented unique proprietary technology that is intended to allow for the licensing and manufacture of a commercially viable self-chilling beverage container. NTI is currently in the development stage of its business. NTI is in the process of taking its planned product from the conceptual stage of development to the production of a prototype of a self-chilling beverage container that can be used for testing purposes. If the testing efforts are successful, the company will then proceed to the marketing phase of the company's plan of operation, which involves marketing the self-chilling beverage container to beverage manufacturers. NTI has not completed the development of a commercially viable self-chilling beverage container to date, nor has it achieved any revenues to date.

A United States patent for a self-chilling beverage container and parts therefor was obtained by a founding stockholder on March 11, 1997. During 1998, the patent and patent holder rights thereunder were sold to the company for \$1. Subsequent costs in June 1999 of \$24,000 to file foreign patent applications have been similarly capitalized.

The company has entered into an exclusive licensing agreement with Balsam Ventures, Inc., dated for reference November 30, 2003, granting Balsam the exclusive right and license, for a period of 40 years, to use, commercialize, and exploit the company's proprietary trademarks, patents, process information, technical information, designs, and drawings associated with the company's self-chilling beverage container technology including the right to manufacture, use, and sell apparatus and products embodying the technology within the countries comprising the European Union and the Republic of China. Balsam also has the right to sub-license the right to manufacture, use, and sell products embodying the technology.

The consideration for the agreement was as follows:

1. Balsam issued to the company 5,000,000 restricted shares of its common stock; and
2. Balsam must pay the company the following royalties:

    a. a sales royalty equal to 2% of gross profits from sales of all apparatus incorporating the technology and/or commercial goods or products incorporating the technology;
    b. a license royalty equal to 5% of revenues received by Balsam from sub-licensing the technology; and
    c. a minimum royalty payment of $5,000 per month commencing on January 15, 2006, which is to be credited towards all royalty payments under the agreement that have been paid by Balsam or become payable by Balsam during the course of the Agreement.

Source: Norpac Technologies, Inc., 2006, 10KSB.

PACKAGING—$335,000 PLUS 2% ON SALES

Advanced Oxygen Technologies, Inc. incorporated in Delaware in 1981 under the name Aquanautics Corporation, was, from 1985 until May 1995, a development-stage specialty materials company producing new oxygen-control technologies.

Advanced Oxygen Technologies Inc. said it has entered into a definitive agreement with W.R. Grace & Co. to sell its proprietary oxygen-control technology. The deal calls for $335,000 in cash and a 2% royalty for the next 12 years on sales of products incorporating the company's technology. Advanced Oxygen Technologies said it expects most of Grace's near term efforts will be focused in the area of oxygen scavenging for food and beverage packaging. This technology removes residual oxygen from packages, contributing to overall freshness of food and beverages, the company said. Specific applications include crowns and closures for bottled foods and beverages, bag-in-box fitments and bags, plastic films and coatings for cans and aseptic packages. The company said that following the sale its only material assets will be its status as a publicly held corporate shell and its net operating loss carryforward, which approximated $22 million at June 30, 1994.

Source: Advanced Oxygen Technologies, Inc., 2001, 10KSB.

PACKAGING—20% OF SALES

EarthShell Corporation licensed its packaging technology to Sweetheart Cup, giving Sweetheart Cup the exclusive right to manufacture and sell EarthShell packaging products in North America. The two companies signed the deal for a 10-year period. This agreement enables Sweetheart to become the primary supplier of EarthShell Packaging plates, bowls, cups, and hinged-lid sandwich containers in North America, and closely follows the announcement of separate agreements signed in the last 90 days with DuPont and Green Earth Packaging. During the first five years, the two companies have set incremental sales goals, finishing with a sales goal of $500 million annually. EarthShell's standard licensing structure provides for a 20% royalty payment on sales of EarthShell Packaging. Sweetheart Cup will purchase the capital equipment necessary to manufacture EarthShell plates, cups, bowls, and hinged-lid sandwich containers.

EarthShell Corporation is an environmental packaging technology company that licenses its products for commercialization. EarthShell packaging is designed to be environmentally friendly, created by combining starches and inorganic materials such as limestone to form cups, plates, bowls and hinged-lid containers and sandwich wraps. Sweetheart Cup Co. began in 1911 as an ice cream cone bakery in Massachusetts. The company has evolved over the years to be the largest manufacturer of single-use disposable food and beverage containers. Still a privately owned company, Sweetheart Cup operates 19 manufacturing and warehouse facilities across the United States and Canada. In Canada the products are sold under the name Lily Cups.

Source: *Licensing Economics Review*, October 2002.

POCKET SHOT ENERGY DRINK—1.5% TO 7% ON SALES

In 2015, Pocket Shot Inc. granted to PS Ventures, Inc. a worldwide, exclusive right and license to use the licensed trademark in connection with the manufacture, distribution, sale, and advertising of the licensed products in the licensed territory. Simultaneously herewith, PS Ventures has issued to Pocket Shots 200,000 shares of Licensees common stock. The licensed trademark is Pocket Shot Energy®, a registered trademark.

Pocket Shot is engaged in the design, production, and distribution of hard liquors and other beverages in flexible single-serving pouches. This agreement pertains to the food and beverage industry relating to energy drinks.

Licensed products means an energy drink enhanced with vitamins, minerals, nutrients, and caffeine and contained in a stand-up plastic pouch approved by Pocket Shot that conforms to the specifications for ingredients and the dimensions and appearance of the plastic pouch; or any other nutritional drink that is non-alcoholic.

In consideration for the rights granted to it under this agreement, the licensee agrees to pay licensor a percentage royalty as follows: 7% of the net sales price on all sales of the licensed products by the licensee to its customers or distributors up to the first 3 million in annual sales; 5% royalty on all sales greater than 3 million in any annual sales cycle and less than 7 million in annual sales; 3% royalty on all sales greater than 7 million in any annual sales cycle and less than 10 million in annual sales; 1.5% royalty on all sales greater than 10 million in any annual sales with no limit.

Source: Pocket Shot Co., 2016, S-1.

S&W AND IL CLASSICO TRADEMARKS—2% ON SALES

On February 4, 2004, Del Monte Corp. granted an exclusive license to Coffee Holding Co. Inc. to use the licensed marks solely in the United States and solely on and in connection with the production, manufacture, distribution, and sale of roasted whole bean and ground coffee for distribution at the retail distribution level.

Del Monte is the owner of the trademarks S&W, IL CLASSICO, and S&W. Del Monte is a North American food production and distribution company.

Licensed Trademarks:
Mark Registration No. Registration Date
S&W and Design 338,457 September 8, 1936
S&W and Design 1,302,906 October 30, 1984
S&W and Design 1,810,987 December 14, 1993
IL CLASSICO 1,816,052 January 11, 1994

The license does not include the right to use the marks on or in connection with any other products or activity and does not include the right to use the marks outside of the United States.

Coffee Holding acknowledged that use of the marks by Del Monte on a global Internet web site or successor technology to identify products sold outside the United States does not violate the agreement.

This license shall commence as of the date of this Agreement and continue for an initial term of ten (10) years ending at the close of business on December 31, 2014.

In consideration for the license granted herein, Coffee Holding agreed to pay Del Monte royalties as follows:

i. Annual royalties on Net Sales of the Products at the rate of 2% of annual Net Sales,
ii. A minimum annual royalty for each contract year (the "Minimum Annual Royalty"), as follows: Year 1: $25,000 Year 2: $25,000 Year 3: $25,000 Year 4: $25,000 Year 5-10: $50,000.

Source: A Coffee Holding Co. Inc., 2004, 10QSB.

SLIM JIM AND PENROSE TRADEMARKS – $11 MILLION

The Slim Jim and Penrose trademarks were valued as part of an acquisition at over $11 million. Goodmark Foods, Inc. announced the completion of its obligations under a 10-year licensing agreement with General Mills. At the conclusion of the license agreement, Goodmark Foods exercised its option to purchase the Slim Jim and Penrose trademarks. Payments during the licensing term, which began with the management buy-out of Goodmark Foods in 1982 from General Mills, totaled $11 million of royalties.

Goodmark Foods is the nation's leading producer and marketer of meat snacks. The company is also a regional producer of packaged meat products, cookies, crackers, brownies, and other snacks. Its principal brands include Slim Jim, Penrose, Pemmican, and Smokey Mountain meat snacks.

The purchase option has required a final payment $500,000. Acquisitions that involved a payment schedule for trademarks based on royalties were used in the 1980s as a tax-reduction strategy. Instead of paying a lump sum at the time of the transaction for trademarks, which wouldn't be amortizable for tax purposes, a royalty payment schedule was agreed to by both parties for a set period of time along with an agreement to pay a final lump-sum (token amount). Since the royalty payments represent tax deductions the strategy turned the acquisition of a trademark into a tax deduction.

SLIM SLAMMER MILK—0.25% OF SALES

In June 2005, Bravo Foods International Corp. (licensee) extended its licensing agreement with Diabetes Research Institute (licensor) to June 30, 2007. The licensed intellectual property consists of a logo plus design on the labels of the Slim Slammers™ product line.

Bravo Foods introduced Slim Slammers® Fortified Milk, a low-calorie version of its Slammers® Fortified Reduced Fat Milk. Slim Slammers® Fortified Milk has no added sugar and is sweetened with sucralose, a natural sweetener made from sugar. Slim Slammers® Fortified Milk is made from 1% fat milk, is fortified with 11 essential vitamins, and is available in the same flavors as the Slammers® brand.

Bravo Foods will pay the Diabetes Research Institute a royalty rate of 0.25% of net sales per this extended license agreement.

Source: Bravo Foods International Corp., 2006, SB-2/A.

SUNKIST, VLASIC, FRENCH'S, AND TABASCO TRADEMARKS—3% TO 5% OF SALES

Sugar Foods, Inc. is a specialty packager and distributor of individual portions of condiments including lemon juice, mustard, relish, mayonnaise, and salad dressing. The company has expanded its business by differentiating its products through the licensing of trademarks that are displayed on the individual packages. The company has licenses to use the names Sunkist, Vlasic, French's, and Tabasco. A typical contract with a trademark owner runs for 10 years with options to renew. Most of the time no up-front fee is paid. Sugar Foods pays for the products that it uses in preparing the individual portion packages plus a royalty fee that runs between 3% and 5% of sales.

SWEET 'N LOW—7% ON SALES

Meridian Holdings, Inc. and Cumberland Packing, Corp. restructured a license agreement in January of 1999 between Old Fashioned and Cumberland allowing Old Fashioned an exclusive license to the Sweet 'N Low brand for promoting, publicizing, advertising, marketing, selling, and distribution in connection with their Syrup within the United States and Canada. In exchange for the use of the trademark, Old Fashioned will pay a royalty of 7% of net sales of their Syrup to Cumberland. The minimum royalty payment per year begins with $20,000 in 1999 and increases $10,000 per year until it reaches $110,000 in the tenth year of the agreement in 2008. If the agreement is renewed after 10 years, in the eleventh year the minimum royalty will be $150,000 and will increase $10,000 dollars each additional year thereafter. In addition, Meridian will issue Cumberland a warrant to purchase up to 350,000 shares of Meridian common stock at a share price of $2.50 or 50% of the average closing trading price for the 20-day period before they can be exercised.

Cumberland Packing, Corp. is the maker of sugar substitute Sweet'N Low. In addition to Sweet 'N Low, Cumberland also makes another sugar substitute, a salt substitute, butter-flavored granules, and "Sugar in the Raw." The company is family owned and based out of Brooklyn, New York.

Meridian Holdings, Inc. was incorporated in 1994 as the surviving entity in a merger with MHI Telecommunications. After the merger the shareholders of Meridian authorized the company to raise working capital and to acquire an operating business. In 1999 Meridian acquired and became the sole shareowner of Old Fashioned Syrup Company, Inc. Old Fashioned is in the business of developing and marketing a sugar-free and fat-free chocolate syrup product. The company is now known as Championlyte and was the first to introduce a sugar-free beverage into the sports drink market.

TOBACCO—2% OF SALES

Star Scientific, Inc. is a technology-oriented tobacco company with a mission to reduce toxins in tobacco leaf and tobacco smoke. The company is engaged in:

1. the development, implementation, and licensing of scientific technology for the curing of tobacco so as to substantially prevent the formation of carcinogenic toxins present in tobacco and tobacco smoke, primarily the tobacco-specific nitrosamines (TSNAs);
2. the manufacturing, sales, marketing, and development of very low-nitrosamine smokeless tobacco products that also carry enhanced warnings beyond those required by the Surgeon General, including ARIVA compressed powdered tobacco cigarette pieces, Stonewall Hard Snuff and Stonewall dry snuff; and
3. the manufacture and sale of discount cigarettes.

Through its StarCured tobacco curing program in the period 1999–2003, the company purchased or arranged for the purchase of very low-TSNA flue-cured tobacco (cured by farmers using the StarCured tobacco curing process), for resale to B&W. Historically, the vast majority of the company's revenues have been generated through the sale of its discount cigarettes, which are currently sold under the following brands: SPORT, MAINSTREET, and G-SMOKE. In 2004, in order to consolidate its brands, the company phased out the VEGAS brand.

Star has continued to manufacture and sell its discount cigarette brands, and the company expects cigarette sales to be its most significant source of revenue for the foreseeable future, notwithstanding its long-term focus on low-TSNA smokeless tobacco products. Star's cigarettes are sold through approximately 129 tobacco distributors throughout the United States, although the company has sought to focus sales efforts in the states of Florida, Minnesota, Mississippi, and Texas, where it does not incur escrow obligations under the tobacco Master Settlement Agreement (MSA).

Star Scientific's long-term focus continues to be the research, development, and sale of products that expose adult tobacco users to lower levels of toxins. The company's overall objective is to ultimately reduce the range of serious health hazards associated with the use of smoked and smokeless tobacco products. The company fully accepts the evidence that links smoking tobacco with a variety of diseases and premature death and believes that it is highly unlikely that the health risks of smoked tobacco can be completely eliminated. Star believes it was the first company to state unequivocally that "there is no such thing as a safe cigarette," and to affix to the back of the package of its first premium low-TSNA product, Advance, a package "onsert" that contained not only scientifically verified comparative content data, but also additional health warnings. Nevertheless, in a world where an estimated 1.2 billion people smoke and use other conventional tobacco products, there is an urgent need to reduce the toxicity of tobacco products to the maximum extent possible, given available technology. Accordingly, the company believes that it has a corporate responsibility to continue to expand its research and development efforts to manufacture tobacco products in the least hazardous manner possible, given available technology, particularly through the StarCured tobacco curing process. However, the company has deferred research projects due to its cost-cutting efforts in the last half of 2003 and 2004 and its current concentration of its resources and efforts on the trial of its patent infringement litigation against R.J. Reynolds Tobacco Company (RJR), the first phase of which was tried before the Court during the period January 31 to February 8, 2005. The extent of future research efforts will depend, in part, on the results of the RJR litigation.

The company has an exclusive, worldwide license from Regent Court Technologies, LLC under 11 patents issued and patents pending relating to methods to substantially prevent the formation of TSNAs in tobacco, including the StarCured tobacco curing process and the production of very low-TSNA tobacco products. The StarCured tobacco curing process involves the control of certain conditions in tobacco curing barns, and in certain applications, uses microwave and/or electronic beam technology. The StarCured process substantially prevents the formation in the tobacco leaf of the carcinogenic TSNAs, which are widely believed by medical and scientific experts to be among the most abundant and powerful cancer-causing toxins present in tobacco and in tobacco smoke.

The company currently markets three very low-TSNA products: (1) ARIVA, a compressed powdered tobacco "cigalett"; (2) Stonewall Hard Snuff, a non-fermented, spit-free™ "hard tobacco" product for moist snuff users; and (3) on a very limited basis, a dry snuff product under the name Stonewall. The tobacco in each of the company's smokeless products is 100% StarCured very low-TSNA tobacco. Previously, the company had manufactured a low-TSNA moist snuff (Stonewall moist snuff). With the introduction of Stonewall Hard Snuff, the company discontinued the manufacture of Stonewall moist snuff. To date, these products have not generated significant revenues.

Star entered into a license agreement as the licensee with Regent Court Technologies, LLC, of which Jonnie R. Williams, the company's founder and Chief Executive Officer and Francis E. O'Donnell, Jr., MD, the beneficiary of the O'Donnell Trust, which is the company's second-largest shareholder (after Mr. Williams), are the owners. The license agreement provides, among other things, for the grant of an exclusive, worldwide, irrevocable license to the company, with the right to grant sublicenses, to make, use, and sell tobacco and products containing tobacco under the licensor's patent rights and know-how relating to the processes for curing tobacco so as to significantly prevent the formation of certain toxic carcinogens present in tobacco and tobacco smoke, namely the tobacco-specific nitrosamines (TSNAs), and to develop products containing such tobacco, whether such patent rights and know-how are now in existence or hereinafter developed.

The company is obligated to pay to Regent Court a royalty of 2% on all net sales of products by it and any affiliated sublicensees, and 6% on all fees and royalties received by it from unaffiliated sublicensees, less any related research and development costs incurred by the company. The license agreement expires with the expiration of the last of any applicable patents. Eleven United States patents have been issued, and additional patent applications are pending in the United States and in approximately 80 foreign jurisdictions. To date, the company has paid no royalties under the license agreement. The license agreement may be terminated by the company upon 30 days' written notice or by Regent Court if there is a default in paying royalties or a material breach by the company or the purchase of Star Scientific's stock or assets.

Source: Star Scientific, Inc., 2005, 10K.

TEA MANUFACTURER—2% OF SALES

In 1998, Honest Tea was founded to fill a niche no one else was targeting. Beverage companies go after the same target market——14- to 18-year-old boys with big bladders and infinite metabolism rates. For a normal person, who doesn't want something that tastes like liquid candy, there was nothing out there.

The secret of Honest Tea's taste is that it's brewed with real tea leaves in spring water, and only lightly sweetened. A 16-ounce bottle has between 18 and 34 calories, depending on the flavor. By contrast, a 16-ounce bottle of Snapple's bestselling Lemon Tea has 200 calories, the equivalent of 13 teaspoons of sugar. Other tea makers use powders or concentrates.

One of Honest Tea's unique offerings is First Nation's Peppermint. After months of negotiation and a consultation with the tribal elders of the Crow Indian Nation, the company developed an organic herbal tea in conjunction with a woman-owned company based on the Crow Reservation in Montana. This tea is exciting, not only for its flavor, but also for the partnership developed with the tribe. In addition to licensing the flavor and artwork from the tribe, Honest Tea is also buying the tea from the Crow Indians on the reservation with the understanding that over time the community will develop the capacity to grow all the ingredients on the reservation.

Honest Tea will pay a royalty of 2% to the Crow Indians, some of it dedicated to a foundation for foster children on the reservation.

Source: Marc Gunther, "Brewed at Yale, Honest Tea Thirsts for Success," *Fortune*, July 10, 2000.

"THIRST AID" SLOGAN—$10.3 MILLION

Quaker Oats Co. must pay for using a Vermont company's trademark to sell its Gatorade sports drink but not the nearly $27 million ordered by a lower court, a federal appeals court ruled. The court agreed that Quaker should pay $10.3 million for using the "Thirst Aid" slogan owned by a Vermont-based company. The appeals court also awarded more than $6 million in interest. A lower court had figured the total award by calculating royalties that might have been paid by Quaker. It then doubled the figure as a deterrent. But the 7th Circuit Court of Appeals said federal trademark law does not allow for penalties in trademark-infringement lawsuits, and ordered the U.S. District Court to reconsider the award. Quaker used the slogan "Gatorade is Thirst-Aid" in national advertising from 1984 to 1990. Sands, Taylor and Woods has owned the "Thirst-Aid" trademark since the early 1920s and used it to sell various soda fountain drinks.

Source: *Licensing Economics Review*, August 1994.

THROWDOWN®—10% OF SALES

In a license agreement effective October 10, 2014, Throwdown Industries Holdings, LLC granted to DeThrone Royalty Holdings, Inc. the exclusive, non-sublicenseable, and non-assignable right, to use the trademarks and other IP solely in connection with the development, manufacture, distribution, marketing, and sale of one or more sports performance drinks.

Throwndown's principal business activity is the design, development, and worldwide marketing and selling of functional equipment, training gear, apparel, and accessories for the impact sports market and fitness industry.

"Sports Performance Drinks" are defined as "[a]ll non-alcoholic beverages designed to give a consumer enhanced physiological and/or performance effects and containing, vitamins, herbal ingredients, and/or other similar ingredients."

The territory of the license is the United States and Canada, and no other areas are granted or guaranteed at this time or in the future.

During the term of the license royalties of 10% of net revenue are due.

Source: DeThrone Royalty Holdings, Inc., 2013, Form 8-K.

UNWIND BEVERAGE – $0.60 FOR EVERY 24 CANS AND $0.12 PER 12-PACK

Frontier Beverage Company, Inc. operates in two main segments within the live entertainment business, including live music events and talent booking services with continued development of beverage products. Frontier Beverage Company, Inc. continues with the development, marketing, and distributing of New Age/Alternative Beverages and snack products. "New Age/Alternative Beverages" is an industry categorization for a group of products that include energy drinks/infused water, fruit juices and drinks, dairy and dairy substitutes, and bottled/canned teas.

On March 1, 2010, the company entered into a Purchase Agreement with Innovative Beverage Group Holdings, Inc., a Nevada corporation, for the purchase of the intellectual property rights for UnWind, which was created and developed by Innovative. In conjunction with the Purchase Agreement, the parties executed a Trademark Assignment, which was filed with the United States Patent and Trademark Office (the "USPTO") assigning us rights to trademarks for "UnWind Extreme Relaxation" and "UnWind."

Under the terms of the Purchase Agreement, the company purchased (i) all rights to the UnWind flavor, including all rights to the proprietary formula used to manufacture UnWind; (ii) the UnWind name and trademark, and all other trademarks, service marks, copyrights, patents, and other intellectual property associated therewith; and (iii) all documentation used in and/or necessary for the manufacture and marketing of the UnWind beverage, including but not limited to manufacturing instructions, ingredient lists, and marketing literature or similar material created for UnWind (the "Purchased Property").

As consideration for the Purchased Property, we agreed to pay Innovative or its assigns: (i) $0.60 for every 24 cans or bottles (or such other beverage container in which Frontier chooses to sell the UnWind product) of the UnWind flavor brand, and (ii) $0.12 per 12-pack box of any additional delivery system of the UnWind flavor brand (and/or any beverages developed using any of the intellectual property rights included in the Purchased Property) that the Company sells during each fiscal quarter.

Source: Frontier Beverage Company, Inc., 2013, 10K.

UNIVERSITY OF TEXAS AT AUSTIN WATER—8% OF SALES

In 2013, the University of Texas at Austin licensed its trademark and logo for use on bottles of drinking water. Logo Waters, Inc. also obtained the rights from the Collegiate Licensing Company to use the University of Texas at Austin's logo and other Texas universities' logos, such as Texas Tech and Texas A&M. The schools and Logo Waters have an agreement whereby the universities will receive an 8% royalty fee on all bottles of water sold, that sport the school logo.

Source: *San Antonio Business Journal*, March 14, 2003.

VERYFINE TRADEMARKS—$513,500

Veryfine Products, Inc., a manufacturer and seller of juice drinks, was awarded $513,500 by the U.S. District Court for the District of Puerto Rico. Colon Brothers, Inc. was found guilty of copying the trademarks and trade dress of Veryfine and was permanently enjoined from infringing the distinctive labels and bottling of the plaintiff. The court based its findings on, among other things, Boston Athletic Association v. Sullivan, 867 F.2d at 29 (1st Cir. 1989).

In the case, eight factors identified for consideration in determining likelihood of confusion including:

1. similarity of marks;
2. similarity of the goods;
3. relationship between parties' channels of trade;
4. relationship between parties' advertising;
5. classes of prospective purchasers;
6. evidence of actual confusion;
7. defendant's intent in adopting its mark; and
8. strength of the plaintiff's mark.

WARNER BROS. BEVERAGES—3% OF SALES

On January 1, 1999, Warner Bros. granted to China Peregrine Food Corp. a non-exclusive right in the licensed territory to use and reproduce the licensed material only on and in connection with the manufacture, advertising, distribution, and sale of the licensed articles. China Peregrine specifically understands and agrees that no rights are granted herein in respect of the Warner Bros. "shield" name or logo, the Warner Bros. Consumer Products name or logo, or the Warner Bros. Studio Store name or logo. The licensed ended on June 30, 2002.

The representations, names, logos, movements, personalities, artwork, photographs and other material in connection with the following "LOONEY TUNES" characters: BUGS BUNNY, TWEETY, SYLVESTER, DAFFY DUCK, TASMANIAN DEVIL, WILE E. COYOTE, ROAD RUNNER, LOLA BUNNY, and MARVIN THE MARTIAN only.

China Peregrine acknowledges that the rights granted are limited only to the cartoon characters set forth above and that any and all rights in, to or associated with the theatrical motion picture entitled "Space Jam," as well as with any sequels thereto or subsequently produced television series, are specifically excluded.

The licensed articles are beverages branded using the licensed material as set forth.

Licensed Articles for distribution in Shanghai:

1. Fresh white milk packaged in gable top cartons (sizes 240, 500, and 950 ml).
2. Fresh flavored milk packaged in gable top cartons (sizes 240, 500, and 950 ml). Flavors: chocolate, vanilla, orange, pineapple, and strawberry.
3. Fresh flavored yogurt drinks packaged in gable top cartons (sizes 500 and 950 ml). Flavors: vanilla, strawberry and orange; other flavors as approved by Licensor.
4. Aseptic (boxed) UHT treated white milk and flavored milk in size 225 ml. Flavors: chocolate, vanilla, orange, pineapple, and strawberry.
5. Reconstituted fruit-flavored juices/beverages packaged in gable top cartons (sizes 240, 500, and 950 ml) or aseptic packaging in 225 ml size. Fruit flavors: orange, apple, peach, pineapple, strawberry, grape, orange/banana blend, and apple/grape blend.

Licensed Articles for distribution in Hangzhou:

1. Fresh white milk packaged in gable top cartons (sizes 250, 500, and 1000 ml) and baggies in size 200 ml. Baggies for distribution only through reserve system in Hangzhou.
2. Fresh flavored milk packaged in gable top cartons (sizes 250, 500, and 1000 ml) and baggies in size 200 ml. Flavors: chocolate, vanilla, orange, pineapple, and strawberry.
3. Fresh flavored yogurt drinks packaged in gable top cartons (sizes 500 and 950 ml) and in glass bottles in size 350 ml. Flavors: vanilla, strawberry, and orange; other flavors as approved by Licensor.
4. Aseptic (boxed) UHT treated white milk and flavored milk in size 225 ml. Flavors: chocolate, vanilla, orange, pineapple, and strawberry
5. Reconstituted fruit-flavored juices/beverages packaged in gable top cartons (sizes 250, 500, and 1000 ml) or aseptic packaging in 225 ml size. Fruit flavors: orange, apple, peach, pineapple, strawberry, grape, orange/banana blend, and apple/grape blend.

Compensation involves the payment by the licensee of 3% of the net invoiced price of each licensed article.

Source: China Premium Food Corp., 2001, SB-2/A.

WATER FILTERING—2% OF SALES

Seychelle Environmental Technologies, Inc. designs and manufactures unique, state-of-the-art Ionic Adsorption Micron Filters that remove up to 99.8% of all pollutants and contaminants found in any freshwater source. Using breakthrough technology, Seychelle has also developed proprietary ozone systems. Patents or trade secrets cover all proprietary products. Since the human body is 75% water and the quality of water worldwide continues to deteriorate, Seychelle's mission is twofold: First, to help educate everyone to the fact that the quality of water they drink is important and second, to make available low-cost, effective filtration products that will meet the growing need for safe water.

Seychelle has sold over two million portable water filtration bottles throughout the world to customers such as individuals, dealers, distributors, governments, military, agencies, and emergency relief organizations, such as the U.S. Marine Corps, the International Red Cross, Eco-Challenge, Kenya Wild Life Service, La Cruz Roja de Mexico, and the NY Institute for the Blind. In addition, the company has donated thousands of portable bottles to church groups and missionaries worldwide. Seychelle's products are approved for sale and distribution in many countries including the United States, Mexico, Brazil, Argentina, Venezuela, Japan, China, Korea, India, Pakistan, Australia, the UK, New Zealand, Malaysia, Indonesia, and South Africa.

In 2001, the World Bank placed the value of the world water market at close to $1 trillion annually. Bottled water, according to Water Facts, has emerged as the second-largest commercial beverage category by volume in the United States. However, Seychelle products compete in a more limited market: the portable and home filtration products segments.

In developing countries, many people in rural areas boil their water for drinking and cooking to kill bacteria, but this process does not remove the pyrogens, chemicals, toxins, and other elements that remain in the water. In Africa alone, according to Earth Prayers from around the world, approximately 6,000 people die every day because of water-borne diseases.

Seychelle signed a license agreement with Aqua Gear USA on June 6, 2002, for a product known as the "Hand Held Pump Technology." Seychelle licensed all proprietary rights associated with this technology. Seychelle pays a 2% royalty on the gross income derived from the license for the technology during the term of the license, which is a pressure patent for a pressure system.

Source: Seychelle Environmental Technologies, Inc., 2006, 10KSB.

WATER TECHNOLOGY—$0.30 TO $0.60 PER CASE

Jacobson Resonance Enterprises, Inc. is in the developmental stage. They are developing electromagnetic resonance technology (Jacobson Resonance) focusing initially on healthcare. The company is planning to use Jacobson Resonance for the reduction of chronic and acute pain, commencing with magneto therapy for the knee. Jacobson Resonance utilizes extremely weak physiologic (like those found in the human heart, brain, and other organs), low frequency electromagnetic fields to beneficially alter molecular characteristics. The company plans to use joint venture and licensing arrangements, as well as its own resources, to develop, manufacture, distribute, and market various applications of Jacobson Resonance.

In January 2000, the company executed a licensing agreement with RealPure Beverage Group, LLC, of Jackson, Mississippi, for the use of Jacobson Resonance in multiple water and beverage products lines, including marketing and distribution. Previously, Benvenutti Electrical Apparatus & Repair built a new industrial model of the Jacobson Resonator for us consisting of three coils, each 10 feet in diameter, placed vertically and connected in series for water resonation. RealPure will use this machine to resonate its water products. The beverages scheduled for resonation include RealPure spring water, as well as a new pediatric beverage, a new geriatric beverage, and the new "Real Pro" hi-energy sport drink. The company's agreement with RealPure gives RealPure the exclusive license in the United States to use the resonance technology for beverages and the right to sublicense these rights, in exchange for a royalty of $.30 per case for resonated water, $.50 per case for resonated sports drinks, $.60 per case for the resonated pediatric drink, and $.45 per case for the resonated geriatric drink.

Resonated water might also lead to the development of energy-efficient home water purification systems by providing a cleaner, less toxic environment and by preventing calcium and other mineral deposits that restrict pipes and damage appliances. Preliminary research testing at the University of Oklahoma has shown that resonated water may enhance the rate of growth of mung beans and soybeans. Other potential agricultural applications include enhancing the health and growth cycles of fish and shellfish, rice farming, forestry and lumber operations, greenhouse facilities, citrus production, wine production, and landscaping.

Source: Jacobson Resonance Enterprises, Inc., 2001, 10KSB.

WATER TECHNOLOGY—1% TO 5% OF SALES

Capacitive Deionization Technology Systems, Inc., in January 1997, entered into a manufacturing and marketing license agreement with Lawrence Livermore National Laboratories (Lawrence Livermore) whereby the company obtained the rights to Lawrence Livermore's patented Capacitive Deionization Technology (CDT). The manufacturing and marketing license is effective for the life of the patents, with most such patents expiring by the year 2016. To maintain the license the company must make contracted minimum annual royalty payments to Lawrence Livermore, in the amount of $25,000 per year. The company will owe Lawrence Livermore royalty payments varying from 1% of product revenue to a maximum of 5% of product revenue. The company is also liable to reimburse Lawrence Livermore for foreign patent filing fees. These fees are incurred by Lawrence Livermore as patents are filed and renewed in foreign countries. During 2004, these fees totaled over $71,000. Although the company is the only licensee for water applications using the carbon aerogel technology, which is the basis of the company's capacitive deionization technology, the license is non-exclusive in that Lawrence Livermore could license other entities to use some or all of the technology covered by the existing license with the company. However, any such license would be limited to Lawrence Livermore technology as it existed in 1996 and would not reflect any enhancements made by the company. The company originally named its product a "brick," but in 2003 filed an application to trademark the name "AquaCell.

The company's capacitive deionization technology, or CDT, uses deionization to convert a contaminated water supply into a "clean" water stream and a separate waste stream. As implemented by the company, the technology involves coating pairs of electrodes with a carbon coating known as carbon aerogel. The carbon aerogel is porous and has an extremely high ratio of ion collection area to surface area, due to the structure of the aerogel. The ion collection area presented by carbon aerogel is greater than 60,000 times the surface area of the electrode. In the company's system, a salt water or impure water stream is passed through an electrostatic field established between pairs of electrodes coated with carbon aerogel. The negative electrode attracts positively charged ions such as chloride or nitrate. Those ions are pulled out of suspension of the water stream and held by the electrodes in the carbon aerogel, until either the power is turned off or the electrode charge is reversed. As a result, with a relatively low application of energy, the company's technology is able to remove a wide variety of contaminants or other molecules from a water stream through the creation and holding of charged particles.

The Lawrence Livermore license authorizes the company to enhance, manufacture, and market CDT, specifically in the fields of:

- Brackish water and seawater conversion
- Industrial and agriculture ground water remediation
- Pure water for boiler applications
- Ultra pure water for manufacturing
- Nuclear waste remediation
- Medical applications

The aerogel product licensed from Lawrence Livermore Laboratories in January 1997 operated at low voltage levels (compatible with solar energy sources) with resulting favorable operating economics; however, the cost of manufacture with the original Lawrence Livermore technology was too expensive to be commercially competitive. Company efforts have been focused on cost reduction programs, which also have improved the operational efficiency of the technology while reducing the manufacturing costs. Systems were also developed that allow the waste stream to access both sides of carbon aerogel, as opposed to the single side of carbon aerogel accessible in the Lawrence Livermore technology. The company is continuing to develop proprietary improvements to further reduce the cost of the manufacturing process and improve the efficiencies.

Source: Capacitive Deionization Technology Systems, Inc., 2005 10KSB.

WATER TECHNOLOGY—$300,000 PLUS 5% TO 7.5% OF SALES

In January 2003, Universal Communications Systems, Inc. identified a new business venture, abandoned the telecommunication and wireless business, and adopted a new business plan. UCS formed a wholly owned subsidiary, AirWater Corporation, whose purpose and mission is to design, build, and market machines that produce drinkable water from the air. The first step in the endeavor was to obtain licensing rights to the technology. To that end, AirWater acquired the rights to four patents by an agreement dated March 24, 2003, relating to this technology from J. J. Reidy Company of Holden, Massachusetts. AirWater Patents Corporation was formed to hold the acquired licensed patent rights. Under the terms of the agreement, AirWater paid $300,000, and is obligated to pay, for a one-year period, a royalty payment of between 5% and 7.5% on all sales of equipment that use the patented technology. Of the $300,000 purchase price, the company paid $100,000 in cash, and the balance of $200,000 was settled by issuing 4,000,000 restricted common shares.

Source: Universal Communication Systems, Inc., 2005, 10KSB,

WILL ROGERS WATER—3% OF SALES

In 2001, Fiesta obtained a license to use Will Rogers' name and a reproduction of one of his museum's paintings on the label of water bottled. Will Rogers was an American cowboy, vaudeville performer, humorist, newspaper columnist, social commentator, and stage and motion picture actor.

In exchange for using Will Rogers' name and a reproduction of one of his museum's paintings on the label, Fiesta will pay a 3% royalty to the foundation.

Source: AP Worldstream SECTION: International News, March 9, 2001.

YOPLAIT YOGURT TRADEMARK—$400,000 PLUS 3% OF SALES

Yolplait Yogurt has licensed its name for the Malaysian market for an upfront license fee of $400,000 plus 3% of sales. Fraser & Neave Holdings acquired the exclusive rights to make and sell Yoplait products in the Malaysian market.

FOOD & BEVERAGE INDUSTRY PROFIT MARGINS. To put the royalty rate data just reported in context, the following information describes key players in the food and beverage industries and presents their most recent operating profit margins.[5]

Publilcy Traded Food Company Profits

Company	Operating Profit Margin
Treehouse Foods	4.47%
Post Holdings	12.47%
Conagra Brands	15.66%
B&G Foods	16.02%
General Mills	17.37%
Campbell Soup	17.78%
Pinnacle Foods	18.16%
Kellogg Company	19.14%
Hershey Company	21.41%
Average	15.83%

Food Industry Participants. **B&G Foods, Inc.** manufactures, sells, and distributes a portfolio of shelf-stable and frozen foods in the United States, Canada, and Puerto Rico. Its products include frozen and canned vegetables, hot cereals, fruit spreads, canned meats and beans, bagel chips, spices, seasonings, hot sauces, wine vinegars, maple syrups, molasses, salad dressings, pizza crusts, Mexican-style sauces,

5. Company descriptions and profit margins have been obtained from Yahoo Finance.

dry soups, taco shells and kits, salsas, pickles, peppers, tomato-based products, puffed corn and rice snacks, cookies and crackers, nut clusters, and other specialty products. The company markets its products under various brands, including Ac'cent, B&G, B&M, Back to Nature, Baker's Joy, Bear Creek Country Kitchens, Brer Rabbit, Canoleo, Cary's, Cream of Rice, Cream of Wheat, Devonsheer, Don Pepino, Durkee, Emeril's, Grandma's Molasses, Green Giant, JJ Flats, Joan of Arc, Las Palmas, Le Sueur, MacDonald's, Mama Mary's, Maple Grove Farms of Vermont, Molly McButter, Mrs. Dash, New York Flatbreads, New York Style, Old London, Original Tings, Ortega, Pirate's Booty, Polaner, Red Devil, Regina, Sa-són, Sclafani, Smart Puffs, SnackWell's, Spice Islands, Spring Tree, Sugar Twin, Tone's, Trappey's, TrueNorth, Underwood, Vermont Maid, Victoria, Weber, and Wright's. It also sells, markets, and distributes household products under the Static Guard brand. B&G Foods, Inc. sells and distributes its products directly, as well as through a network of independent brokers and distributors to supermarket chains, food service outlets, mass merchants, warehouse clubs, non-food outlets, and specialty distributors. The company was formerly known as B&G Foods Holdings Corp. and changed its name to B&G Foods, Inc. in October 2004. B&G Foods, Inc. was founded in 1996 and is headquartered in Parsippany, New Jersey.

Campbell Soup Company, together with its subsidiaries, manufactures and markets branded food and beverage products. It operates through three segments: Americas Simple Meals and Beverages, Global Biscuits and Snacks, and Campbell Fresh. The Americas Simple Meals and Beverages segment engages in the retail and food service of Campbell's condensed and ready-to-serve soups; Swanson broth and stocks; Prego pasta sauces; Pace Mexican sauces; Campbell's gravies, pastas, beans, and dinner sauces; Swanson canned poultry products; Plum food and snack products; V8 juices and beverages; and Campbell's tomato juices in the United States, Canada, and Latin America. The Global Biscuits and Snacks segment provides Pepperidge Farm cookies, crackers, bakery, and frozen products in the United States retail; Arnott's biscuits in Australia and Asia Pacific; and Kelsen cookies worldwide, as well as simple meals and shelf-stable beverages in Australia and the Asia Pacific. The Campbell Fresh segment offers Bolthouse Farms fresh carrots, carrot ingredients, refrigerated beverages, and refrigerated salad dressings; Garden Fresh Gourmet salsa, hummus, dips, and tortilla chips in the United States; and refrigerated soups. The company sells its products through retail food chains, mass discounters and merchandisers, club stores, convenience stores, drug stores, and dollar stores, as well as other retail, commercial, and non-commercial establishments; and independent contractor distributors. Campbell Soup Company was founded in 1869 and is headquartered in Camden, New Jersey.

Conagra Brands, Inc., together with its subsidiaries, operates as a food company in North America. The company operates through Grocery & Snacks, Refrigerated & Frozen, International, and Foodservice segments. The Grocery & Snacks segment primarily offers shelf-stable food products in various retail channels in the United States. The Refrigerated & Frozen segment provides temperature-controlled food products in various retail channels in the United States. The International reporting segment offers food products in various temperature states in retail and foodservice channels outside of the United States. The Foodservice segment offers food products, including meals, entrees, sauces, and various custom-manufactured culinary products packaged for sale to restaurants and other foodservice establishments in the United States. Conagra Brands, Inc. sells its products under the Marie Callender's, Reddi-wip, Hunt's, Healthy Choice, Slim Jim, Orville Redenbacher's, Alexia, Angie's BOOMCHICKAPOP, Blake's, Duke's, Frontera, Banquet, Chef Boyardee, and BIGS brand names. The company was formerly known as ConAgra Foods, Inc. and changed its name to Conagra Brands, Inc. in November 2016. Conagra Brands, Inc. was founded in 1919 and is headquartered in Chicago, Illinois.

General Mills, Inc. manufactures and markets branded consumer foods worldwide. The company operates in five segments: North America Retail; Convenience Stores & Foodservice; Europe & Australia; Asia & Latin America; and Pet. It offers ready-to-eat cereals, refrigerated yogurt, soup, meal kits, refrigerated and frozen dough products, dessert and baking mixes, frozen pizza and pizza snacks, grain, fruit, and savory snacks, as well as organic products, including refrigerated yogurt, nutrition bars, meal kits, salty snacks, ready-to-eat cereal, and grain snacks. It also supplies branded and unbranded food products to the North American foodservice and commercial baking industries; and manufactures and markets pet food products, including dog and cat food.

The company markets its products under the Annie's, Betty Crocker, Bisquick, Blue Buffalo, BLUE Basics, BLUE Freedom, BLUE Wilderness, Bugles, Cascadian Farm, Cheerios, Chex, Cinnamon Toast Crunch, Cocoa Puffs, Cookie Crisp, EPIC, Fiber One, Food Should Taste Good, Fruit by the Foot, Fruit Gushers, Fruit Roll-Ups, Gardetto's, Go-Gurt, Gold Medal, Golden Grahams, Häagen-Dazs, Helpers, Jeno's, Jus-Rol, Kitano, Kix, La Salteña, Lärabar, Latina, Liberté, Lucky Charms, Muir Glen, Nature Valley, Oatmeal Crisp, Old El Paso, Pillsbury, Progresso, Raisin Nut Bran, Total, Totino's, Trix, Wanchai Ferry, Wheaties, Yoki, and Yoplait trademarks. General Mills sells its products directly, as well as through broker and distribution arrangements to grocery stores, mass merchandisers, membership stores, natural food chains, e-commerce retailers, commercial and noncommercial foodservice distributors and operators, restaurants, convenience stores, and pet specialty stores, as well as drug, dollar, and discount chains. It operates 507 leased and 372 franchise-branded ice cream parlors. The company was founded in 1866 and is based in Minneapolis, Minnesota.

The Hershey Company, together with its subsidiaries, manufactures and sells confectionery products. The company operates through two segments, North America; and International and Other. It offers chocolate and non-chocolate confectionery products; gum and mint refreshment products comprising mints, chewing gums, and bubble gums; pantry items, such as baking ingredients, toppings, beverages, and sundae syrups; and snack items, including spreads, meat snacks, bars and snack bites, mixes, popcorn and protein bars, and cookies. The company provides its products primarily under the Hershey's, Reese's, Kisses, Jolly Rancher, Almond Joy, Brookside, barkTHINS, Cadbury, Good & Plenty, Heath, Kit Kat, Lancaster, Payday, Rolo, Twizzlers, Whoppers, York, Scharffen Berger, Dagoba, Ice Breakers, Breathsavers, and Bubble Yum brands, as well as under the Golden Monkey, Munching Monkey, Pelon Pelo Rico, IO-IO, Nutrine, Maha Lacto, Jumpin, Sofit, SkinnyPop, Oatmega, Paqui, and Tyrrells brands. It markets and sells its products to wholesale distributors, chain grocery stores, mass merchandisers, chain drug stores, vending companies, wholesale clubs, convenience stores, dollar stores, concessionaires, and department stores. The Hershey Company was founded in 1894 and is headquartered in Hershey, Pennsylvania.

Kellogg Company, together with its subsidiaries, manufactures and markets ready-to-eat cereal and convenience foods. The company operates through U.S. Morning Foods, U.S. Snacks, U.S. Specialty, North America Other, Europe, Latin America, and Asia Pacific segments. Its principal products include cookies, crackers, savory snacks, toaster pastries, cereal bars, granola bars and bites, fruit-flavored snacks, ready-to-eat cereals, frozen waffles, and veggie foods. The company offers its cereals and cereal bars under the Kellogg's brand, as well as under the Kashi and Bear Naked brand; frozen foods under the Eggo and Morningstar Farms brands; and cookies, crackers, crisps, and other convenience foods under the Kellogg's, Keebler, Cheez-It, Pringles, Murray, Austin, and Famous Amos brands. The company sells its products for retailers through direct sales forces, as well as use brokers and distributors in approximately 180 countries. Kellogg Company was founded in 1906 and is headquartered in Battle Creek, Michigan.

Pinnacle Foods Inc. manufactures, markets, and distributes branded convenience food products in North America. It operates through four segments: Frozen, Grocery, Boulder, and Specialty. The Frozen segment offers frozen vegetables, frozen complete bagged meals, frozen prepared seafood, frozen and refrigerated bagels, frozen pizza, and full-calorie single-serve frozen dinners and entrées under the Birds Eye, Birds Eye Voila!, Van de Kamp's, Mrs. Paul's, Lender's, Celeste, Hungry-Man, and Aunt Jemima brand names. The Grocery segment provides cake/brownie mixes and frostings, cookie mixes, shelf-stable salad dressings, salad dressings, canned meat, table syrups, margarine/spread, pie and pastry fruit fillings, barbecue sauce, and shelf-stable pickles under the Duncan Hines, Vlasic, Wish-Bone, Western, Armour, Brooks, Nalley, Log Cabin, Mrs. Butterworth's, Smart Balance, Comstock, Wilderness, and Open Pit brands. The Boulder segment offers gluten-free products, natural frozen meal offerings, plant-based refrigerated and shelf-stable spreads, and plant-based protein frozen products under the Udi's, Glutino, EVOL, Earth Balance, and Gardein brands. The Specialty segment provides snack products under the Hawaiian kettle style chips, Tim's Cascade, Snyder of Berlin, and Husman's brand names; and manufactures and distributes products primarily in the gluten-free, frozen meat substitutes, canned meat, and pie and pastry fruit filling categories, as well as engaging in private label businesses. The company sells its products through supermarkets, grocery wholesalers and distributors, mass merchandisers, super centers, convenience stores, dollar stores, natural and organic food stores, drug stores, warehouse clubs, and e-commerce websites in the United States and Canada, as well as in military channels and foodservice locations. Pinnacle Foods Inc. is headquartered in Parsippany, New Jersey.

Post Holdings, Inc. operates as a consumer packaged goods holding company in the United States and internationally. It manufactures and sells ready-to-eat cereal and hot cereal, egg, refrigerated potato, cheese and other dairy case, and pasta products; and markets and distributes ready-to-drink beverages, bars, powders, and other nutritional supplements. The company also manufactures peanut butter and other nut butters, baking nuts, dried fruits, and nuts; distributes cereals and snacks; and provides peanut blanching, granulation, and roasting services to the peanut industry. The company markets its products under various trademarks, including Post, Honey Bunches of Oats, Great Grains, Post Shredded Wheat, Spoon Size Shredded Wheat, Golden Crisp, Alpha-Bits, Oh's, Shreddies, Post Raisin Bran, Grape-Nuts, Honeycomb, Frosted Mini Spooners, Golden Puffs, Cinnamon Toasters, Fruity Dyno-Bites, Cocoa Dyno-Bites, Berry Colossal Crunch, Malt-O-Meal, Farina, Dyno-Bites, MOM's Best, Better Oats, CoCo Wheats, Weetabix, Barbara's, Puffins, Snackimals, Attune, Uncle Sam, Erewhon, Willamette Valley Granola Company, Peace Cereal, Sweet Home Farm, Crystal Farms, All Whites, Papetti's, Better'n Eggs, Easy Eggs, Emulsa, Table Ready, Davidson's Safest Choice, Abbotsford Farms, Simply Potatoes, Diner's Choice, Crescent Valley, Westfield Farms, David's Deli; Premier Protein, Joint Juice, Dymatize, ISO.100, Supreme Protein, PowerBar, Golden Boy, Golden Organics, Country Orchard, Weetabix, Alpen, Weetos, Ready Brek, Weetabix On the Go, and Oatbix. It sells products to grocery, mass merchandise, supercenters, club store, and drug store customers; military, e-commerce, and foodservice channels; foodservice distributors, restaurant chains, retail grocery stores, and food manufacturers and processors; and foodservice and food ingredient customers through internal sales staff, broker organizations, and direct sales forces. The company was founded in 1895 and is headquartered in St. Louis, Missouri.

TreeHouse Foods, Inc. operates as a food and beverage manufacturer in the United States, Canada, and Italy. The company operates through Baked Goods, Beverages, Condiments, Meals, and Snacks segments. The Baked Goods segment offers candies, cookies, crackers, in-store bakery products, pita chips, pretzels, refrigerated dough, retail griddle waffles, pancakes, and French toasts. The Beverages segment offers broths, liquid non-dairy creamers, non-dairy powdered creamers, powdered drinks, single serve hot beverages, specialty teas, and sweeteners. The Condiments segment offers cheese and pudding products; jams, preserves, and jellies; mayonnaise; Mexican, barbeque, and other sauces; pickles and related products; refrigerated and shelf-stable dressings and sauces; and table and flavored syrups. The Meals segment offers baking and mix powders; powdered soups and gravies; macaroni and cheese; pasta; ready-to-eat and hot cereals; skillet dinners; and condensed and ready to serve soup and infant feeding products. The Snacks segment offers bars, dried fruits, snack nuts, trail mixes, and other wholesome snacks. The company sells its products through various distribution channels comprising grocery retailers and foodservice distributors, as well as food manufacturers and repackagers of foodservice products. TreeHouse Foods, Inc. was founded in 1862 and is based in Oak Brook, Illinois.

Beverage Industry Participants.

Publilcy Traded Beverage Company Profits

Company	Operating Profit Margin
Cott Corporation	3.57%
Arca Continental	11.38%
Embotelladora Andina S.A.	11.80%
Coca-Cola FEMSA, S.A.B. de C.V.	12.72%
Pepsi	16.65%
Dr. Pepper Snapple	20.36%
National Beverage	21.05%
The Coca-Cola Co.	27.14%
Monster Beverage	36.63%
Average	17.92%

Arca Continental, S. A. B. de C. V., together with its subsidiaries, manufactures, distributes, and sells non-alcoholic beverages in the United States, Mexico, Argentina, Peru, and the Republic of Ecuador. It operates through Beverages and Other segments. The company's products include soft drinks, water, dairy drinks, juices, nectars, sports drinks, energy drinks, tea, carbonated and not carbonated drinks, low-calorie drinks, and vitamin drinks, as well as snacks and candies. It sells its soft drink products under the brands owned or licensed by The Coca-Cola Company; and food and snack products under the Bokados, Inalecsa, and Wise brands, as well as value-added dairy products under the ToniCorp brands. The company was formerly known as Embotelladoras Arca, S. A. B. de C. V. Arca Continental, S. A. B. de C. V. is headquartered in Monterrey, Mexico.

The Coca-Cola Company, a beverage company, manufactures and distributes various nonalcoholic beverages worldwide. The company provides water, enhanced water, and sports drinks; juices; juice, dairy, and plant-based beverages; teas and coffees; and energy drinks. It also offers concentrates, syrups, beverage bases, source waters, and powders/minerals, as well as fountain syrups to fountain retailers, such as restaurants and convenience stores. The company sells its products primarily under the Coca-Cola, Diet Coke/Coca-Cola Light, Coca-Cola Zero Sugar, Fanta, Sprite, Minute Maid, Georgia, Powerade, Del Valle, Schweppes, Aquarius, Minute Maid Pulpy, Dasani, Simply, Glacéau Vitaminwater, Gold Peak, FUZE TEA, Glacéau Smartwater, Ice Dew, I LOHAS, and Ayataka brand names. The Coca-Cola Company offers its beverage products through a network of company-owned or controlled bottling and distribution operators, as well as through independent bottling partners, distributors, wholesalers, and retailers. The company was founded in 1886 and is headquartered in Atlanta, Georgia.

Coca-Cola FEMSA, S.A.B. de C.V., a franchise bottler, produces, markets, distributes, and sells Coca-Cola trademark beverages. The company offers a portfolio of products, including sparkling beverages, still beverages, juices, sports, and energy drinks, as well as teas, waters, isotonics, and dairy products. It provides a portfolio of approximately 154 brands directly, as well as through retail outlets and restaurants to consumers in Mexico, Guatemala, Nicaragua, Costa Rica,

Panama, Colombia, Venezuela, Brazil, and Argentina. The company was founded in 1979 and is headquartered in Mexico City, Mexico.

Cott Corporation, together with its subsidiaries, operates as a route based service company in North America and Europe. It operates in three segments: Route Based Services; Coffee, Tea and Extract Solutions; and All Other. The company's product portfolio includes bottled water, coffee, brewed tea, water dispensers, coffee and tea brewers, specialty coffee, liquid coffee or tea concentrate, single cup coffee, cold-brewed coffee, iced blend coffee or tea beverages, blended teas, hot tea, sparkling tea, coffee or tea extract solutions, filtration equipment, hot chocolate, soups, malt drinks, creamers/whiteners, cereals, beverage concentrates, and mineral water. It provides its services to residences, businesses, restaurant chains, hotels and motels, small and large retailers, and healthcare facilities. The company serves approximately 2.4 million customers or delivery points through its platform, sales and distribution facilities, and fleets, as well as through wholesalers and distributors. Cott Corporation was incorporated in 1955 and is based in Mississauga, Canada.

Dr. Pepper Snapple Group, Inc. manufactures and distributes non-alcoholic beverages in the United States, Mexico and the Caribbean, and Canada. The company operates through three segments: Beverage Concentrates, Packaged Beverages, and Latin America Beverages. It offers flavored carbonated soft drinks (CSDs) and non-carbonated beverages (NCBs), including ready-to-drink teas, juices, juice drinks, mineral and coconut water, and mixers, as well as manufacturing and selling Mott's apple sauces. The company sells its flavored CSD products primarily under the Dr. Pepper, Canada Dry, Peñafiel, Squirt, 7UP, Crush, A&W, Sunkist soda, Schweppes, RC Cola, Big Red, Vernors, Venom, IBC, Diet Rite, and Sun Drop; and NCB products primarily under the Snapple, Hawaiian Punch, Mott's, FIJI, Clamato, Bai, Yoo-Hoo, Deja Blue, ReaLemon, AriZona tea, Vita Coco, BODYARMOR, Mr. & Mrs. T mixers, Nantucket Nectars, Garden Cocktail, Mistic, and Rose's brand names. It serves bottlers and distributors, and retailers. Dr. Pepper Snapple Group, Inc. was incorporated in 2007 and is headquartered in Plano, Texas.

Embotelladora Andina S.A., together with its subsidiaries, produces, markets, and distributes Coca-Cola soft drinks in Chile, Brazil,

Argentina, and Paraguay. It also offers fruit juices, ready-to-drink tea, other fruit-flavored beverages, and mineral and purified water; and flavored waters and other carbonated beverages. In addition, the company distributes non-carbonated beverages, such as tea, fruit juices, energy and sport drinks, and waters; beer under the Amstel, Bavaria, Birra Moretti, Desperados, Dos Equis (XX), Edelweiss, Heineken, Kaiser, Sol, and Xingú brands; and spirits. Further, it manufactures glass and polyethylene terephthalate bottles, cases, and plastic caps. The company offers its products primarily through small retailers, restaurants and bars, supermarkets, and third-party distributors. Embotelladora Andina S.A. was founded in 1946 and is headquartered in Santiago, Chile.

Monster Beverage Corporation, through its subsidiaries, develops, markets, sells, and distributes energy drink beverages, soda, and its concentrates in the United States and internationally. It operates through three segments: Monster Energy Drinks, Strategic Brands, and Other. The company offers ready-to-drink packaged drinks, non-carbonated dairy-based coffee and energy drinks, and non-carbonated energy shakes primarily to bottlers and full service beverage distributors, as well as selling directly to retail grocery and specialty chains, wholesalers, club stores, drug stores, mass merchandisers, convenience chains, food service customers, and the military; and concentrates and/or beverage bases to authorized bottling and canning operations; and ready-to-drink packaged energy drinks to bottlers and full service beverage distributors. Monster Beverage Corporation sells its products under the Monster Energy, Monster Energy Ultra, Monster Rehab, Monster Energy Extra Strength Nitrous Technology, Java Monster, Muscle Monster, Punch Monster, Juice Monster, Übermonster, BU, Mutant Super Soda, Monster Hydro, Espresso Monster, Caffé Monster, Nalu, NOS, Full Throttle, Burn, Mother, Ultra Energy, Play and Power Play(stylized), Relentless, BPM, Gladiator, and Samurai brands. The company was formerly known as Hansen Natural Corporation and changed its name to Monster Beverage Corporation in January 2012. Monster Beverage Corporation was founded in 1985 and is headquartered in Corona, California.

National Beverage Corp., through its subsidiaries, develops, produces, markets, and sells a portfolio of flavored beverage products in North America and internationally. The company offers beverages to active and health-conscious consumers, including sparkling waters under the LaCroix, LaCroix Cúrate, LaCroix NiCola, and Shasta Sparkling Water brand names; energy drinks and shots under the Rip It brand name; juice and juice-based products under the Everfresh, Everfresh Premier Varietals, and Mr. Pure brand names; and carbonated soft drinks in various flavors comprising regular, sugar-free, and reduced-calorie options under the Shasta and Faygo brands. It serves retailers, as well as various up-and-down-the-street accounts through the take-home, convenience, and food-service distribution channels. The company sells and markets its products through an internal sales force, as well as specialized broker networks. National Beverage Corp. was founded in 1985 and is based in Fort Lauderdale, Florida. National Beverage Corp. is a subsidiary of IBS Partners, Ltd.

PepsiCo, Inc. operates as a food and beverage company worldwide. Its Frito-Lay North America segment offers Lay's and Ruffles potato chips; Doritos, Tostitos, and Santitas tortilla chips; and Cheetos snacks, branded dips, and Fritos corn chips. The company's Quaker Foods North America segment provides cereals, rice, pasta, mixes and syrups, granola bars, grits, oat squares, oatmeal, rice cakes, simply granola, and side dishes under the brands Quaker, Aunt Jemima, Cap'n Crunch, Life, Quaker Chewy, and Rice-A-Roni. Its North America Beverages segment offers beverage concentrates, fountain syrups, and finished goods under the Aquafina, Diet Mountain Dew, Diet Pepsi, Gatorade, Mist Twst, Mountain Dew, Pepsi, Propel, and Tropicana brands; and ready-to-drink tea, coffee, and juices. The company's Latin America segment provides snack foods under the Cheetos, Doritos, Emperador, Lay's, Marias Gamesa, Rosquinhas Mabel, Ruffles, Sabritas, Saladitas, and Tostitos; cereals and snacks under the Quaker brand; and beverage concentrates, fountain syrups, and finished goods under the 7UP, Diet Pepsi, Gatorade, H2oh!, Manzanita Sol, Mirinda, Pepsi, and Toddy brands. Its Europe Sub-Saharan Africa segment offers snack food; cereals and snacks; beverage concentrates, fountain syrups, and finished goods; ready-to-drink tea products; and dairy products under the Agusha, Chudo, and Domik v Derevne brand names. The company's Asia, Middle East, and North Africa segment provides snack foods under the Cheetos, Chipsy, Crunchy, Doritos, Kurkure, and Lay's brands; cereals and snacks under the Quaker brand; beverage concentrates, fountain syrups, and finished goods; and ready-to-drink tea products. The company was founded in 1898 and is headquartered in Purchase, New York.

THE 25% RULE. In Chapter 17, "Use of the 25% Rule in Valuing Intellectual Property," beginning on page 272, licensing royalty rate guidance can be obtained from this general rule of thumb. As discussed in Chapter 17, in its pure form the rule is as follows. An estimate is made of the licensee's expected profits for the product that embodies the intellectual property at issue. Those profits are divided by the expected net sales over that same period to arrive at a profit rate. That resulting profit rate, say 16%, then is multiplied by 25% to arrive at a running royalty rate. In this example, the resulting royalty rate would be 4%. Going forward (or calculating backward, in the case of litigation), the 4% royalty rate is applied to net sales to arrive at royalty payments due to the intellectual property owner. The licensee/user receives access to the intellectual property, yet the price (i.e., royalty) it pays will still allow it to generate positive product returns.

The theory underlying this rule of thumb is that the licensor and licensee should share in the profitability of products embodying the patented technology or a key trademark. The a priori assumption is that the licensee should retain a majority (e.g., 75%) of the profits because it has undertaken substantial development, operational, and commercialization risks, contributed other technology/intellectual property, and/or brought to bear its own development, operational, and commercialization contributions.

Focus of the rule is placed on the licensee's profits because it is the licensee that will be using the intellectual property.[6] Intellectual property,

---

6. In the reasonable royalty determination in *Standard Manufacturing Co., Inc. and DBP, Ltd. v. United States*, both sides' experts focused on the patent holder's profit rate. The court took exception, noting that defendants' profits were a "more realistic and reliable estimation of profits which were earned to [the plaintiff] by the infringement since they are derived from the actual sale of [the infringing product]." *Standard Manufacturing Co., Inc. and DBP, Ltd. v. United States*, 42 Fed. Cir. 748, 767 (1999). The court noted that a variety of federal courts held the same, citing *Mahurkar v. C. R. Bard., Inc., Davol Inc.*, and *Bard Access System, Inc.*, 79 F.3d 1572, 1580 (Fed. Cir. 1996) (district court did not err in calculating portion of award when it initially used infringer's profit rate); *TWM Manufacturing Co., Inc. v. Dura Corp. and Kidde, Inc.*, 789 F. 2d 895, 899 (Fed. Cir. 1986) (affirming district court's computation of damages based on infringer's profits); *Trans-World Manufacturing Corp. v. Al Nyman & Sons, Inc. and Al-Site Corporation*, 750 F. 2d 1552, 1568 (among factors considered in determining reasonable royalty was the infringer's anticipated profit from the invention's use and evidence of infringer's actual profits probative of anticipated profit).

like any other asset, derives its value from the use to which it will be put.[7] Focus also is placed on expected profits because the license negotiation is meant to cover forthcoming and ongoing use of the intellectual property.[8] It is the expected benefits from use of the intellectual property that will form the basis for the licensee's payment of an access fee. Past, or sunk, costs typically should be ignored because a decision is being made about the future.[9] That is, what going-forward price results in the product being a sound investment? Any product in which the projected marginal benefits exceed the projected marginal costs should be undertaken.

The rule places focus on fully loaded profits because they measure the (accounting) returns on a product. Gross profits represent the difference between revenues and manufacturing costs. Gross profits, however, do not account for all of the operating expenses associated with product activity. Those costs include marketing and selling, general and administrative, and research and development expenses. Some of those costs are associated directly with product activity; others are common across product lines.

"Fully loaded" profits account for the fact that a variety of nonmanufacturing overhead expenses are undertaken to support the product activity, even though they may not be linked directly to certain volume or activity levels. Such costs are often driven by product activity. Failure to take into account these operating expenses may lead to an overstatement of the returns associated with the sales of a product.

Fully loaded profits may refer either to pretax profits or to operating profits. Pretax profits are calculated as revenues minus (1) cost of goods, (2) nonmanufacturing overhead expenses, and (3) other income and expenses. The historical relationships underlying the 25% rule, however, have in fact been between royalty rates and operating profits. The latter is revenues minus (1) cost of goods sold and (2) nonmanufacturing

7. In some circumstances, the *licensor's* profits may provide some guidance. That is, those profits may, in part, reflect his or her appetite for a license, and those profits may serve as a surrogate for missing or unknown licensee profits.

8. Razgaitis, *Early-Stage Technologies* (New York: John Wiley & Sons, 1999), p. 108. *Fonar Corporation and Dr. Raymond V. Damadian v. General Electric Company and Drucker & Genuth, MDs, P.C. d/b/a South Shore Imaging Associates*, 107 F.3d 1543 (Fed. Cir. 1997). *Hanson v. Alpine Valley Ski Area, Inc.*, 718 F.2d 1075 (Fed. Cir. 1983).

9. Richard Brealey and Stewart C. Myers, *Principles of Corporate Finance*, sixth ed. (New York: McGraw-Hill, 2000), p. 123.

overhead. Other income and expenses are not subtracted out. In many cases, these two measures of profit are quite similar; in other cases, they are not. Given that the value of intellectual property is independent of the way in which a firm (or project) is financed, from a theoretical point of view, the operating profit margin is the correct measure to use.

Royalty guidance for this new section can be obtained by application of the 25% multiple factor times the average operating profit margins developed for the food and beverage industry.

For the food industry, operating profits for the selected public companies averaged 15.83%. Multiplied by 25% indicates a royalty rate of just under 4% of net sales. For the beverage industry, the selected public companies reported an operating profit margin of 17.92%. When multiplied by 25%, a 4.5% royalty rate is indicated.

These rates are approximately in the middle of the range established by the rates charted previously in this new section. Specific royalty-rate data that differs from those indicated by the 25% rule reflect specific profits margins expected from licensing-specific technology or trademark assets.

This analysis reinforces the general concept that the 25% rule of thumb provides very good guidance for establishing a royalty rate but when possible additional analysis should be sought so that refinement can be introduced reflecting specific circumstances and conditions that are unique to each license negotiation.

INDEX